Multidimensional Programming

Multidimensional Programming

E. A. Ashcroft
Arizona State University

A. A. Faustini
Arizona State University

R. Jagannathan
SRI International, Menlo Park

W. W. Wadge
University of Victoria

New York Oxford
OXFORD UNIVERSITY PRESS
1995

Oxford University Press

Oxford New York
Athens Auckland Bangkok Bombay
Calcutta Cape Town Dar es Salaam Delhi
Florence Hong Kong Istanbul Karachi
Kuala Lumpur Madras Madrid Melbourne
Mexico City Nairobi Paris Singapore
Taipei Tokyo Toronto

and associated companies in
Berlin Ibadan

Published by Oxford University Press, Inc.,
200 Madison Avenue, New York, New York 10016

Library of Congress Cataloging-in-Publication Data
Multidimensional programming /
Edward A. Ashcroft . . . [et al.].
p. cm. Includes bibliographical references and index.
ISBN 0-19-507597-8
1. Lucid (Computer program language).
I. Ashcroft, Edward A.
QA76.73.L83M85 1994 005.13'3—dc20 94-31181

9 8 7 6 5 4 3 2 1
Printed in the United States of America
on acid-free paper

Preface

When Oxford University Press (OUP) first approached us with the idea of writing a book on our recent research, we first thought of putting together a collection of material published in recent International Symposiums on Lucid and Intensional Programming. In fact, this was our initial proposal to OUP. However, the editor(s) suggested that it would be much more appropriate to write about several aspects of a single important development. It was clear to us what this was—the ability to manipulate *multidimensional objects* in Lucid in a natural, implicit, and distributed manner. Therefore this book is about multidimensional declarative programming.

From a historical perspective, the material in this book can be traced back directly to the seminal work of two of the authors, Ed Ashcroft and Bill Wadge (described in "Lucid, a non-procedural language with iteration," Communications of the ACM (July 1977)). Although many features of Lucid were originally considered somewhat obscure, these same features have become more "mainstream" as pointed out in the following excerpt from Paul Whiting and Robert Pascoe's article entitled "A History of Data-Flow Languages" in the IEEE Annals of the History of Computing (Special Issue on Computer Languages), Volume 16, Number 4, 1994.

> many of those aspects of Lucid which were originally regarded as too idiosyncratic to be commonly accepted by programmers are precisely those aspects which are widely accepted in the data-flow community today.

The best known practical derivative of Lucid is the real-time programming language for reactive systems called Lustre, which was developed by N. Halbwachs and others at the IMAG Institute in Grenoble, France and is being applied in developing commercial real-time systems, notably in aerospace.

The work described in this book is the continuation of the original ideas of Ashcroft and Wadge. A significant milestone in the development of this work was the 1985 publication *Lucid: The Dataflow Programming Language.* At that time, it gave readers a snapshot of what were then the latest developments in the Lucid work—mainly its evolution as a dataflow programming language. Since then much of the work has focussed on the often serendipitous consequences of Lucid's intensional logic foundation. Multidimensional declarative programming is one such consequence and its conceptual and applied aspects are the principal focus of this book although we briefly consider other uses of intensionality.

The work described here has been supported by several organizations: The U.S. National Science Foundation (Grants CCR-9203249 and CCR-9203732), the Natural Sciences and Engineering Research Council of Canada, and Mitsubishi Electric Corporation of Japan. Also, SRI International has generously committed its resources in making this book possible.

We would like to thank Don Jackson of OUP, New York for his help and patience. We would also like to thank all our colleagues and students over the years for their many valuable and often pivotal contributions. Notable among them is Calvin Ostrum who as an enthusiastic undergraduate at the University of Waterloo in 1980 single-handedly wrote the first eductive interpreter for Lucid. Finally, we would be remiss if we did not acknowledge our families and friends for their unwavering support.

Ed Ashcroft
Tony Faustini
Jaggan Jagannathan
Bill Wadge

September 1994

Contents

List of Figures

Multidimensional Programming

Chapter 1

Introduction

This book, obviously, is about multidimensional declarative programming. Many different languages and paradigms may be claimed to result in multidimensional declarative programming. We are most concerned with a programming paradigm where the existence of different dimensions (even temporary dimensions) enables algorithms to be expressed naturally. The latest version of the language `Lucid` uses dimensions in this way and we will use `Lucid` throughout most of this book. We will emphasize that `Lucid` is a language that embodies a particular style or paradigm of programming that we call intensional programming. Toward the end of the book there will be a chapter that indicates how other language features and capabilities could fit into this same paradigm. Therefore this book is about multidimensional, declarative, *intensional* programming, with examples given mostly in the latest version of `Lucid`.

`Lucid` has been around since the mid-seventies [7]. Nevertheless, with its new polydimensionality capabilities it provides a fresh approach to programming and, we hope, introduces declarative programming to a whole new audience. In addition, we often find it is useful to think of `Lucid` programs as manipulating geometrical entities, even though programs are actually implemented very simply i.e., without any data structures corresponding to those geometrical entities. Thinking of programs as manipulating geometrical entities adds a visual aspect to programs, while the fact that there are no actual structures in the implementation emphasizes that Lucid programs can be *thought of* in several different ways. We tend to think of programs, and variables in programs, at a very high level when writing programs and ignore the implementation details. Yet for a very high level language, those implementation details are surprisingly simple. Programs are written while thinking of large, multidimensional entities, and yet the implementation deals only with small fragments. In fact, we might modify an environmental movement slogan and say "program globally and implement locally." By the end of the book the appropriateness and meaning of this slogan should be apparent.

This introductory chapter begins by illustrating some of the novelty of the new `Lucid` with a very simple program for transposing a matrix.

The algorithm we use can best be thought of geometrically. We start off with a matrix in the horizontal plane, say, with the `x` dimension going to the right and the `y` dimension coming toward us. (For concreteness, get hold of a micro floppy disk or something similar.) Now, the disk (matrix) is tipped up, away from us, into a new dimension, `t` say, which we assume goes up vertically. The disk is now facing away from us, standing on the edge that used to be furthest from us.

Continuing, we now rotate the disk toward us about its leftmost edge, resulting in the disk facing to the right and still standing on the same edge. Finally, we rotate the disk rightwards about the edge on which it is standing, so that it lies horizontally, face down, and is the transpose of the original horizontal disk, as though it had been flipped over while maintaining the back-left/front-right diagonal in its original position. (See Figure 1.1.)

In a program, all we need to say is that our original matrix, `A`, is realigned three times, in different ways. The realignment is done by the function `realign`, and the program is of the form

```
realign ( realign ( realign ( A ) ) )
```

Actually, we need a little more: we have to say in each case how the matrix is rotated, i.e., how what used to be aligned in one dimension ends up being aligned in another. The function `realign` becomes `realign.a,b`, for example, indicating that elements aligned with dimension `a` become aligned with dimension `b`. The program then becomes

```
realign.t,x ( realign.x,y ( realign.y,t ( A ) ) )
```

The dimension `t` is just a temporary dimension. It is only used to fold things out of the way in the middle of the flipping process. This is a normal thing to do; for example, pancakes cannot be flipped

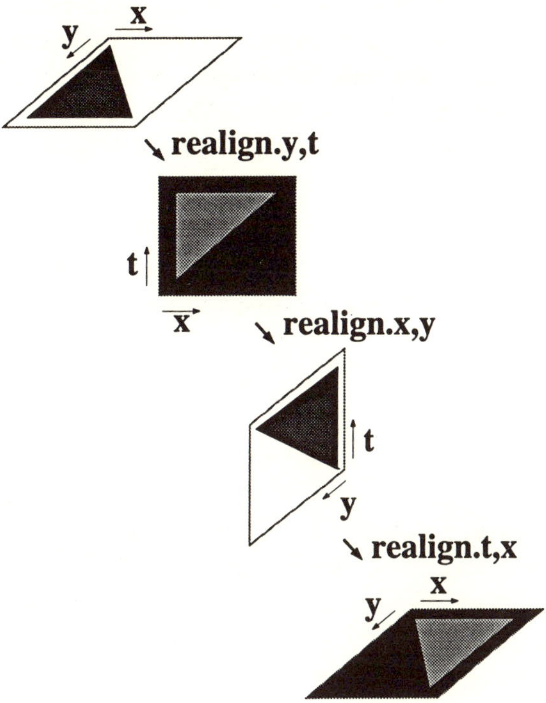

Figure 1.1: Lucid-style Matrix Transposition

over without tossing them into a third dimension, namely, upwards. The program has to be able to tell us that `t` is a new dimension, orthogonal to all others, and that is done by means of a declaration `dimension t`.

The complete Lucid program is therefore

```
realign.t,x ( realign.x,y ( realign.y,t ( A ) ) )
  where
    dimension t;
  end
```

assuming that there is a definition of the function `realign`. (Such a definition will be given very shortly.)

Notice that this matrix transposition program does not use subscripts. Later in this chapter we will see a matrix multiplication program that is equally subscript-free. This ability to program with, and produce, multidimensional objects without the use of subscripts is one of the salient features of Lucid and intensionality. It may appear that this avoidance of subscripts has had the unfortunate effect of wasting space. To construct the transposed matrix it seems we have had to build two other matrices, thereby using three times as much space as was necessary. (Transposing a matrix by using subscripts can usually be done in place.) In fact, the implementation of `Lucid` will not require so much space to be used by this program (see Chapter 5).

Clearly, the matrix-transposition program is easily understood if it is thought of geometrically in the way indicated. Nevertheless, the language is not fundamentally based on geometry; it is based on a form of logic.

Our multidimensional declarative programming is based on intensional logic [43], which is a branch of mathematical logic originally developed to give formal semantics to natural languages. The applicability of intensional logic to declarative programming languages (specifically `Lucid`) was noted by Faustini and Wadge in explaining the original version of the language which, hitherto, had been thought of as a dataflow language [20]. Original `Lucid` programs were defined just over a single dimension that was never named (and was implicit) but which we referred to in discussions as "time." Clearly, `Lucid` has since been generalized to allow arbitrary dimensions, which have to be named [17, 18]. The language fits well with applications that are best understood geometrically, but it also fits with applications, like the *N Body Problem*, in which the geometry of the physical reality being modeled does not correspond directly with the dimensions used in the `Lucid` program that is the solution [6, 2].

In this chapter, several example programs in `Lucid` will be given, explained, and discussed. It is hoped that the examples will intrigue our readers enough to delve into the rest of the book. There, they will find explained the concept of intensionality (Chapter 2). Chapter 3 gives the abstract and concrete syntax of the latest version of the language `Lucid` and it outlines its denotational semantics. The use of `Lucid` as a formal system for program transformation and verification is explored in Chapter 4. For `Lucid` programs to be evaluated correctly and efficiently requires a novel model of computation that is described in Chapter 5. In Chapter 6, we show that this model of computation has enormous potential parallelism and also is naturally endowed with fault tolerance. The language's practicality will be seen in Chapter 7, which is about a high-performance parallel implementation of the model of computation. Multidimensional declarative programming means more than just programming in `Lucid`, however, and this will be made clear in Chapter 8 where ways in which intensionality can be useful in expressing various other programming concepts are explored.

We will now introduce the features of the language by working through several examples of simple applications. The first example, *running sums*, is extremely simple but it introduces the intensional point of view. It also will be used in the later examples.

1.1 Running Sums

The task here is to give the running sums of the values of some variable, say `x`, that varies in dimension `t`. If `x` takes on the values 3, 5, 1, 6, .., for example, the variable that is to hold the running sums, let us call it `s`, takes on the values 3, 8, 9, 15, .. In `Lucid` this is achieved by the following definition of `s`

```
s = x fby.t next.t x + s;
```

(The operation `fby.t` should be read "followed, in the `t` dimension, by" and it has lower priority than the other operations in the definition of `s`, and `next.t` has higher priority, so think of the definition as

```
s = x fby.t ( ( next.t x ) + s );
```

Notice that definitions in `Lucid` are terminated by semicolons.)

This definition should be thought of as defining *all* the values that `s` takes on in dimension `t`—at any point, the value of `s` at the next point in dimension `t` is the value of `x` at the next point in dimension `t` plus the value of `s` at the current point in dimension `t`; at the first point in dimension `t`, the value of `s` is the value of `x` at the first point in dimension `t`. Because the value of `s` at the next point in dimension `t` needs the value of `s` at the *current* point in dimension `t`, the definition is essentially defining an *iterative* and *sequential* computation. (Sequentiality seems to be a necessary property of computations of the *running* sum.) We can think of the value of `s` as a number that *changes* indefinitely. It changes indefinitely because we haven't indicated the point in dimension `t` at which to stop.

There are several ways to think of this definition *operationally*. One way is to think that it generates values spontaneously as long as it is supplied with values for `x`. Another way is to think that it repeatedly gives values provided values are asked for (and it is the asking for particular values of `s` that causes particular values of `x` to be asked for.) The first is the *data-driven* view and the second is the *demand-driven* view. For many reasons, the demand-driven view is the more correct and the more practical [4], and we shall adopt it in this book. Nevertheless, the data-driven view is often useful, especially when we are trying to see what a program *means.* (The meaning of the program is given by the mathematical semantics, which is independent of the method of operationally driving programs, and any way of looking at a program operationally may be useful in gaining an intuitive understanding of the meaning.)

We should think of `s` (and `x`) as having values, individual numbers in this case, that depend on the contexts in which they are demanded. The contexts are just the points, or *indices*, in dimension `t`, of inputs (for `x`) and results (for `s`). (As we will see (Chapter 2), this is the *intensional* point of view in which contexts are indices.) We don't think of `s` as being an infinite object (an infinite sequence laid out in dimension `t`) but rather as being a simple object (a number) that depends on the *index* (the point in dimension `t`). It also is part of the intensional point of view that the index should be implicit as much as possible. (Note that in the definition of `s` there is no *explicit* mention of the index.)

We could equally well have defined `s` to be varying in dimension `a`, and the definition would almost be identical

```
s = x fby.a next.a x + s;
```

These two definitions of `s` are very similar, and the steps in the computations of the values of the two `s`'s are identical. The only differences are whence (from which dimension) the values of `x` are taken and whither (into which dimension) the values of `s` are put. (Both definitions expect `x` and `s` to vary in the same dimension, either both varying in dimension `t` in the first case or both varying in dimension `a` in the second.)

At this point, the reader might be puzzled by a seeming inconsistency in our descriptions of programs. In the earlier *transpose* program, we adopted and recommended a geometrical view in which one thinks of extended objects. Now we say that we "should" think of variables as having values that are just the individual elements of extended objects, not the extended objects themselves. Why are we being so ambivalent?

The point is that there are different ways of viewing programs and the computations of variables. The most general and the most "correct" is the element-by-element approach. In particular cases, however, it is sometimes helpful to view all the elements in one or more dimensions as being grouped together to form an extended object. Then, the variable can be thought of as such an extended object, varying in the other dimensions (the ones whose elements were not grouped together). This constitutes a useful way of gaining an understanding of the program, but the "grouping together" is purely a mental device, it doesn't correspond to anything in the implementation. As we will see, the implementation works elementwise.

We can use the definitions of `s` that we have just given as the bodies of *functions* to compute running sums. The function `runningSumInT` is defined as follows

```
runningSumInT(y) = s where
  s = y fby.t next.t y + s;
end;
```

whereas the function `runningSumInA` is defined as

```
runningSumInA(y) = s where
  s = y fby.a next.a y + s;
end;
```

In fact, the effects of *both* these functions can be obtained from a single "dimensionally abstracted" function definition that uses a formal dimension, in this case `d`.

```
runningSum.d(y) = s  where
  s = y fby.d next.d y + s;
end;
```

If we were to later call `runningSum.a(E)` (i.e., we *focussed* the dimensionally abstracted function `runningSum` onto the dimension `a`), we would get the effect of `runningSumInA(E)`. If we were to call `runningSum.t(E)`, we would get the effect of `runningSumInT(E)`. (Dimensionally abstracted functions were first proposed by Faustini and Jagannathan in [17].)

Although the indices (the positions in dimensions) are usually implicit in programs there are occasions when it is useful to refer to the current value of the index in a particular dimension *explicitly*. To do this we simply use the expression consisting of the operation `#` together with the name of the dimension for which we need the index.

`#.a` refers to the position in dimension `a`. The operation `#` is equivalent to a dimensionally abstracted function (say `position`), which we might define as follows

```
position.d = 0 fby.d position.d + 1;
```

Notice that this definition is very similar to the following definition of the variable `z` that varies in dimension `b`

```
z = 0 fby.b z + 1;
```

Perhaps instead of saying that `position` is a dimensionally abstracted *function*, we should say that it is a dimensionally abstracted *variable* —a variable that varies in whatever dimension we want to specify. If we adopt this terminology, we also should say that `#` is a dimensionally abstracted *constant*, taking the view that variables are nullary functions and constants are nullary operations. In fact, this is exactly what we are going to do.

As an example of the use of `#`, consider the following expression, which has a (free) variable `x`

```
runningSum.b(x)/(#.b + 1)
```

Assume that it is being used in a program at a place where there is no appropriate definition of `x`. What does the expression evaluate to?

It gives us the running *averages* as `x` varies in the `b` dimension. Like any `Lucid` expression it should be thought of as a *recipe* for giving us any one of an arbitrary number of values. To get any one of them we just have to ask for the value of the expression in a specific *context*; in this case, at a specific point in dimension `b`. The value at that point is the average of `x` up to that point, because the recipe just tells us to divide the running sum at that point by `#.b + 1`, the number of elements we have added together so far.

For example, if we want the value at point 3 in dimension `b`, we just divide the value of `runningSum.b(x)`, at point 3 in dimension `b`, by 4, which is the value of `#.b + 1` at point 3 in dimension `b`. How do we get the value of `runningSum.b(x)` at point 3 in dimension `b`? We just evaluate, at point 3 in dimension `b`, the expression defining the function, namely

```
s where
   s = y fby.d next.d y + s;
end;
```

after we first substitute the actual dimension b for the formal dimension d and substitute the actual parameter x for the formal parameter y. In other words we evaluate

```
s where
    s = x fby.b next.b x + s;
  end;
```

at point 3 in dimension b. This, in turn, will cause us to ask for x at point 3 in dimension b and s at point 2 in dimension b. How do we get x at point 3 in dimension b? By our previously stated assumption, the variable x has no definition in the program, so its values have to come from "outside." (It is an *input variable.*) If the value of x at point 3 in dimension b has not already been supplied, the operating system will issue a request for it to the user.

Clearly, we could define a function average as follows

```
average.b(x) = runningSum.b(x)/(#.b + 1);
```

In fact, it would be better if we defined runningSum and average together, as follows

```
{runningSum, average}.b(x) = {s, s/(#.b + 1)} where
   s = y fby.d next.d y + s;
end;
```

The reason it is better to define them with a common body in this way is that recomputation can thereby be avoided. If, for some term E, we ask for the value of runningSum.z(E) in some context, and later we ask for the value of average.z(E) in the same context, the necessary values of s already will have been calculated and stored. They only get calculated once.

The functions defined in this chapter, such as runningSum and average, behave very differently from the functions found in a conventional imperative programming language. The functions can be thought of as being *continuously acting*, that is, "processes," that produce varying results as their arguments vary. (This "process" type of description is an example of a useful data-driven view.) The function also is *nonpointwise*, by which we mean that its result in a particular context doesn't just depend on the value of its argument in that context. (The value of x might be 5 in many different contexts, for example, but at those points the running sums of x will probably be different.)

The functions behave differently in another very important way. We have assumed (in fact, the original statement of the problem implied) that the input variable denoted a sequence of numbers. Amazingly enough, the function, `runningSum`, that we have produced works on more than just sequences of numbers. If the input, `A`, is a `b`-sequence of `a`-sequences, `runningSum.b(A)` we will give us the `b`-sequence of running sums of the `a`-sequences. By that we mean that the `a`-sequences are summed pointwise, so that if `A` is the following sequence of sequences (where dimension `a` goes vertically downwards and dimension `b` goes horizontally rightwards), then

$$\begin{array}{ccccccc} 1 & 3 & 4 & 2 & 7 & \cdot & \cdot \\ 3 & 1 & 6 & 7 & 9 & \cdot & \cdot \\ 1 & 9 & 2 & 1 & 4 & \cdot & \cdot \\ \cdot & \cdot & \cdot & \cdot & \cdot & \cdot & \cdot \\ \cdot & \cdot & \cdot & \cdot & \cdot & \cdot & \cdot \end{array}$$

`runningSum.b(A)` gives the following sequence of running sums of sequences

$$\begin{array}{ccccccc} 1 & 4 & 8 & 10 & 17 & \cdot & \cdot \\ 3 & 4 & 10 & 17 & 26 & \cdot & \cdot \\ 1 & 10 & 12 & 13 & 17 & \cdot & \cdot \\ \cdot & \cdot & \cdot & \cdot & \cdot & \cdot & \cdot \\ \cdot & \cdot & \cdot & \cdot & \cdot & \cdot & \cdot \end{array}$$

How can this be? How can the function work for complicated input when it was designed to work for simple input? The answer is found in the demand-driven evaluation strategy used for intensional programming; if we ask for a value at a point in a two dimensional space, the input will be requested, demanded, in two dimensions. If we ask for `runningSum.b(A)` in a context where the position in dimension `a` is i and the position in dimension `b` is j, the value of the local variable `s` at the same point will be demanded. This will result in demands for `A` at the same point and for `s` at the previous point—i in dimension `a` and j-1 in dimension `b` (assuming that j is greater than 0). The function doesn't mention dimension `a` at all, but that just means that the dimension `a` context doesn't get changed. The function `runningSum.b` will work for arguments of *any* dimensionality. It works in a special way for dimension `b`, and extends pointwise to all the other dimensions.

This way that functions extend happily to higher-dimensioned arguments, giving higher-dimensioned results, when it wasn't originally intended, was noticed in the language `APL` by Ashcroft. It doesn't always work for all arguments in `APL`, but when it does,

Ashcroft said, it was an application of "the Serendipity Principle" [1]. Now, in the later but unrelated language `Lucid`, functions *always* extend, and serendipity really does seem to be the language's underlying principle.

Using the values for `A` that were given previously, the expression `runningSum.a(A)` gives

```
1  3   4   2   7   . .
4  4   10  9   16  . .
5  13  12  10  21  . .
.  .   .   .   .   . .
.  .   .   .   .   . .
```

Interestingly, if we evaluate either `runningSum.a ( runningSum.b(A) )` or `runningSum.b ( runningSum.a(A) )` we get

```
1  4   8   10  17  . .
4  8   18  27  43  . .
5  18  30  40  60  . .
.  .   .   .   .   . .
.  .   .   .   .   . .
```

More interestingly, we can actually *prove* that

```
runningSum.a( runningSum.b(A)) =
                   runningSum.b( runningSum.a(A)),
```

for any `A`, `a`, and `b`. That proof uses the definitions in the program as axioms and the proof technique is conventional mathematics, using a few special properties of the `Lucid` operations, such as `first.p first.q C = first.q first.p C` (and similarly for `next`).

We will now see how `runningSum` can be used in another program.

1.2 Powers

It is well known, and easily checked, that the running sums of the odd positive integers (1, 3, 5, 7, etc.) are the squares (1, 4, 9, 16, etc.). Not so well known is the following generalization, that gives the `N`-th powers for any natural number `N`. (This was pointed out to one of the authors, Ashcroft, by R. Backhouse. See [39].)

This algorithm uses a variable `n` that will be numbers, that starts off as `N`, and also a variable `seq` that will be ordered infinite sequences, that starts off as the sequence of positive integers in order (*all* of them). We successively massage this infinite sequence `seq` and the number `n` as follows. Provided `n` is not 1, we drop off every `n`-th element of `seq`, and find the running sums (*all* of them), giving us a new ordered sequence for `seq`. We then reduce `n` by 1, and repeat the process. If `n` gets to 1 we stop.

Here is a illustration of this algorithm, for `N` = 4. We start off with

```
1 2 3 4 5 6 7 8 9 10 11 12 13 14 15 16 17 18 ...
```

Dropping every fourth, we get

```
1 2 3 5 6 7 9 10 11 13 14 15 17 18 ...
```

Summing, we get

```
1 3 6 11 17 24 33 43 54 67 81 96 113 131 ...
```

We now reduce `n` by one, to 3, and repeat. Dropping every third, we get

```
1 3 11 17 33 43 67 81 113 131 ...
```

Summing, we get

```
1 4 15 32 65 108 175 256 369 500 ...
```

We now reduce `n` by 1, to 2, and repeat. Dropping every second, we get

```
1 15 65 175 369 ...
```

Summing, we get

```
1 16 81 256 625 ...
```

We now reduce `n` by 1, to 1, and repeat. But since `n` is 1, we stop, with, of course, the fourth powers of 1, 2, 3, 4, 5, ...

Notice that if `N` were 2, we would just form the running sums of the odd numbers, namely the squares. As promised, this is a generalization of the conventional way of producing squares.

Since we already know how to do running sums in `Lucid`, perhaps we can "code up" this algorithm. The first thing we realize when we try to code up, is that the algorithm *starts off* with an infinite sequence and then produces more and more sequences, all of them infinite, until we get the desired infinite sequence of `N`-th powers. We generate a sequence of sequences. This fits in perfectly with having two different dimensions, `a` and `b`. We will generate an `a`-sequence `seq` of `b`-sequences of integers.

We can define the sequence `posint` of positive integers, laid out in dimension `b`, as follows

```
posint = 1 fby.b posint + 1;
```

Equivalently, we could have said

```
posint = #.b + 1;
```

or just

```
posint = next.b #.b;
```

However we do it, we can use `posint` as the way that `seq` starts off. The variable `n` starts off as `N` and then is repeatedly decremented, so we already have part of our code

```
seq = posint fby.a .... ;
n = N fby.a n - 1;
```

The final sequence of `N`-th powers will be the sequence `seq` when `n` becomes 1. This means that the general form of the program can be seen to be

```
seq asa.a n eq 1
  where
    dimension a;
    seq = posint fby.a .... ;
    n = N fby.a n - 1;
  end
```

(The operation `asa` should be read as "as soon as.")

The declaration `dimension a;` at the top of the body of the where clause indicates that the dimension `a` is new, and will be used only inside the where clause. It is orthogonal to any other dimensions. (In this case there is only one other dimension, namely `b`.)

Since `n` gets to 1 exactly when the index in the `a` dimension is `N - 1` (since indices start at 0), an equivalent sketch would be

```
seq @.a (N - 1)
  where
    dimension a;
    seq = posint fby.a .... ;
    n = N fby.a n - 1;
  end
```

The very useful operation `@` (pronounced "at", of course) gives us the value of its first argument *at* the position, in the appropriate dimension, specified by the second argument. It works as follows `P @.c q` denotes the value of `P` in the context that differs from the

current one only in that the position in dimension c is the value of q in the current context.
Notice that

```
P @.c #.c = P
```

(Algebraic laws like this one enable formal proofs of program properties to be carried out, and are outlined in Chapter 4.) While we are showing that @ and # sometimes work together, it may be interesting to note that the function realign, used earlier in the matrix transposition program, can be defined as follows

```
realign.a,b(A) = A @.a #.b;
```

From this and the earlier algebraic law we can easily see that

```
realign.c,c(P) = P @.c #.c = P.
```

Other interesting identities are

```
realign.a,b(#.a) = #.b and realign.a,b(#.b) = #.b
```

which together imply that

```
realign.a,b(#.a) = realign.a,b(#.b).
```

To finish off the program, in the definition of seq we just have to say that at each point we get a new b-sequence by dropping off every n-th one and forming the b-sequence of running sums. We do this repeatedly. All we need is a function drop such that drop.d(y, r), say, denotes the sequence y compressed in the d dimension by dropping off every r-th element. (Notice that d is a dummy dimension. When the function is used d will be instantiated as b. Notice also that the first argument of drop is supposed to be a d-sequence whereas the second must not vary in the d dimension. We will only use the function for such a constant (in d) second argument, whatever d actually is.) Given such a function, the definition of seq becomes

```
seq = posint fby.a runningSum.b(drop.b(seq, n));
```

(Notice that n doesn't vary in the b dimension.)

How do we compress a sequence, as drop is required to do? The definition of the function drop must have a formal dimension, say c, the dimension in which we will do the compressing. The first formal parameter will be U and the second will be m. (As we keep on emphasizing, m will be constant in the c dimension.)

First we have to devise a test that will tell us, at each point in dimension `c`, if the corresponding element of the sequence to be compressed is wanted, and then we use this test in an operation that does the compression.

In this example, the test, say `wanted`, will only depend on the position in dimension `c` and the constant `m`. It could be defined as

```
wanted = (#.c + 1) mod m ne 0;
```

This particular definition of `wanted` applies the operation `mod` at every point in dimension `c`. This repeated use of the expensive `mod` operation can be avoided by directly defining an integer sequence `sawtooth` that corresponds to `(#.c + 1) mod m`, as follows

```
wanted = sawtooth ne 0
  where
    sawtooth = 1 fby.c if sawtooth eq m
                       then 0
                       else sawtooth + 1 fi;
  end;
```

Try calculating a few values of `sawtooth` for some numeric value of `m` and you will see that it continually approaches `m`, only to drop back to 0 before it gets there. The values we want correspond to the nonzero values of `sawtooth`.

This second definition of `wanted` *is* more efficient, in that it performs less computation for a given number of results, but the first definition may be preferable in some circumstances because the results can all be computed in parallel. The values of `sawtooth`, on the other hand, have to be computed sequentially.

Whichever definition of `wanted` we decide to use, we must now compress `seq`, using only the elements for which `wanted` is true. The most straightforward way to do this is to use the Lucid operation `wvr` (which can be read "whenever" or "wherever"). We just have to calculate `seq wvr.b wanted`. Choosing, for example, the first definition of `wanted`, we get

```
drop.c(U, m) = U wvr.c wanted
  where
    wanted = (#.c + 1) mod m ne 0;
  end;
```

(The operation `wvr` is equivalent to the following function

```
wvr.c(x, p) =
  if first.c p
     then first.c x fby.c wvr.c(next.c x, next.c p)
     else wvr.c(x, next.c p) fi;
```

It is actually implemented as the following, more efficient, function

```
wvr.c(x, p) = x @.c t2
  where
    t1 = if p then #.c else next.c t1 fi;
    t2 = t1 @.c (t2 + 1)
  end;
```

It picks out from x exactly the elements for which p is true.)

Since there are various choices to be made, there are several possible Lucid programs for this powers-generating algorithm. One of them is

```
seq @.a (N - 1)
  where
    dimension a;
    seq = posint fby.a runningSum.b(drop.b(seq, n));
    posint = next.b #.b;
    runningSum.d(y) = s where
      s = y fby.d next.d y + s;
    end;
    drop.c(U, m) = U wvr.c wanted where
      wanted = (#.c + 1) mod m ne 0;
    end;
    n = N fby.a n - 1;
  end
```

(This program has no input variables.)

1.3 Matrix Multiplication

We will now show how the features of Lucid that we have introduced can be used to define matrix multiplication. In what follows we will define the matrix product of matrix A and matrix B. By "matrix," of course, we just mean an object that varies in two dimensions, say x and y, where going in the x dimension means going down a column and going in the y dimension means going along a row. A matrix will be an x-sequence of rows or, equivalently, a y-sequence of columns. We will assume that A has n columns and B has n rows.

To multiply A and B we have to multiply, pointwise, the rows of A and the columns of B and add together the values produced. More precisely, the *(i,k)*-th element of the product is the sum of the n values

$$A_{i,j} \times B_{j,k}$$

$$\forall j, 1 \leq j \leq n.$$

The required program is just

```
runningSum.z(product) @.z (n - 1)
  where
    dimension z;
      product = realign.y,z(A) * realign.x,z(B);
      realign.u,v(C) = C @.u #.v;
      runningSum.d(y) = s where
        s = y fby.d next.d y + s;
      end;
  end
```

This program works because when *i* is the context, or index, in dimension x, realign.y,z(A) is row number *i+1* of A laid out in temporary dimension z and, when *k* is the index in dimension y, realign.x,z(A) is column number *k+1* of B laid out in temporary dimension z, also. At each point in dimension z, product is then the product of the appropriate elements of the row and column. The whole program returns the sum of the first n such products. (Notice that we use runningSum.z with an argument that is a z-sequence of two-dimensional arrays! We are actually making good use of the Serendipity Principle!)

Perhaps the main interest of this matrix multiplication example is in the way it shows that subscripts are really unnecessary, even for matrix multiplication. Also of interest is the way the program is almost a term in a formal calculus. (There is no recursion involved, and we really could have substituted out the equations, essentially giving such a term

```
runningSum.z(A @.y #.z * B @.x #.z) @.z (n - 1)
  where
    dimension z;
  end
```

Of course, the reason we didn't do that is that the names of the function realign and of the variable product help to explain the program.)

The main drawback of this program for matrix multiplication is the fact that computing `runningSum` is sequential. Apart from that, everything in the program can be done in parallel. With lots of processors, and, perhaps, data-driven evaluation, the running time of the program would be linear in `n`. There *is* a way of improving this: we can use a faster way of summing a set of numbers.

One way of summing numbers quickly is by using a tournament [5]. The idea here is to sum, say, 16 numbers—A_0 through A_{15}—by first adding them together in pairs, *simultaneously*. The eight results are then added together in pairs, simultaneously, then the four results are added in pairs, simultaneously, and then the two "finalists" are added, giving the sum of the complete set of sixteen numbers in *four* steps. The secret to coding it in Lucid is to realize that when a set is divided up into pairs, for adding, the first element of each pair is in an even position (A_0, A_2, A_4, for example) and the second element of each pair is in an odd position (A_1, A_3, A_5, for example). Using the formal dimension `v` to indicate the dimension in which the values to be added are laid out, we can define two useful functions

```
firstOfPair.v(C) = C @.v (#.v * 2);
secondOfPair.v(C) =  C @.v (#.v * 2 + 1);
```

If the values to be added are actually laid out in dimension `u`, at each step we calculate

```
firstOfPair.u(A) + secondOfPair.u(A)
```

Assuming we use a new dimension `t` to lay out the results, `B`, of each step, the new summing function is

```
sum.u(A, n) =
  B @.t (log n)
      where
        dimension t;
        B = A fby.t
              firstOfPair.u(A) + secondOfPair.u(A);
        firstOfPair.v(C) = C @.v (#.v * 2);
        secondOfPair.v(C) =  C @.v (#.v * 2 + 1);
      end;
```

Figure 1.2 illustrates tournament-style summation pictorially. We use `j` to denote to `#.t` and `k` to denote `#.u`.

Using this function, the matrix multiplication program would be

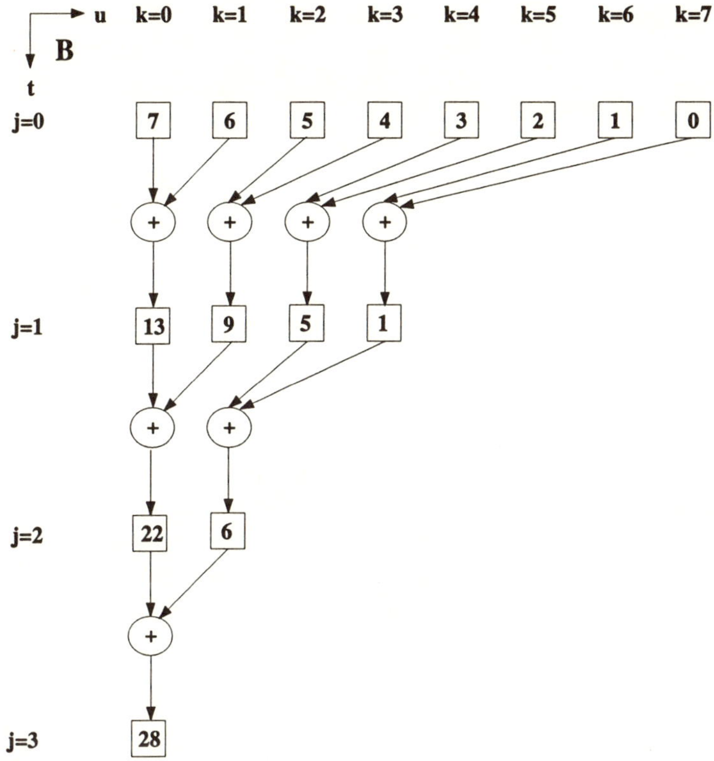

Figure 1.2: Tournament summation example

```
sum.z(product,n)
  where
    dimension z;
    product = realign.y,z(A) * realign.x,z(B);
    realign.u,v(C) = C @.u #.v;
    sum.u(A, n) = B @.t (log n)
      where
        dimension t;
        B = A fby.t
            firstOfPair.u(A) + secondOfPair.u(A);
        firstOfPair.v(C) = C @.v (#.v * 2);
        secondOfPair.v(C) =  C @.v (#.v * 2 + 1);
      end;
  end
```

It would run in time logarithmic in `n`, provided there are enough processors, etc. The function `sum`, and thus the program, requires that the value of `n` be a power of 2, but it can be modified to handle other values.

1.4 Sorting

The idea behind the above tournament for summing numbers can be used for *sorting* numbers. The point is that any operation can be used in a tournament as long as it is *associative*, and the operation of merging sorted lists is clearly associative and it returns sorted lists. (In particular, `merge(A, merge(B, C))` = `merge (merge(A, B), C)`.)

Thus, all we have to do is start with trivial sorted lists of one element each and merge them all, using a tournament, to get all the elements in order.

We start, as suggested, with a `u`-sequence of trivial, one-element `w`-sequences, and use the function `merge` instead of addition. The result will be a trivial, one-element `u`-sequence containing a sorted `w`-sequence. We will return the sorted list as a `u`-sequence.

If we start with a `u`-sequence `A` of elements to sort, how do we get a `u`-sequence of trivial `w`-sequences, each of which contains an element of `A`? We just say `A fby.w eod`. (We indicate the end of a sequence by using a special constant called `eod` ("end of data"). We can detect the end of a sequence by using the test `iseod`. We will use this test shortly in the definition of `merge`.)

Why does the expression `A fby.w eod` do the job, and what is the wonderful property of `Lucid` that told us we would be able to do this so simply? The wonderful property, of course, is intensionality in which data structures are implicit. `A` really isn't a `u`-sequence that we have constructed; all we have are the elements of `A`, and they can themselves be elements of a (conceptual) `w`-sequence. To see that `A fby.w eod` can be thought of as a `u`-sequence of `w`-sequences we just have to see what we get in a context that consists of a position, i, in the `u` dimension and a position, j, in the `w` dimension. If `j` is 0 we get the value of `A` at position i in the `u` dimension - the appropriate element of `A`. If j is greater than 0 we get the value of `eod`. So, if i is fixed, as we increase j, and thus go along the `w`-sequence, we get the element of `A` at position i and then `eod`. That is exactly what we wanted.

The sorting function is as follows

```
sort.u(A, n) =
  realign.w,u(B @.t (log n))
    where
```

```
    dimension t, w;
    B = (A fby.w eod) fby.t
        merge.w(firstOfPair.u(A), secondOfPair.u(A));
    firstOfPair.v(C) = C @.v (#.v * 2);
    secondOfPair.v(C) =  C @.v (#.v * 2 + 1);
  end;
```

It takes the length-n list A in dimension u and returns it sorted in dimension u.

The function merge, and the operation upon, which merge uses, can be defined as follows

```
merge.a(x, y) =
  if iseod yy or xx <= yy then xx else yy fi
  where
     xx = x upon.a iseod yy or xx <= yy;
     yy = y upon.a iseod xx or yy < xx;
  end;
x upon.a p =
  x @.a q
    where
      q = 0 fby.a if p then q + 1 else q fi;
    end;
```

(The name of operation upon is really short for "advanced upon" and it repeats its first argument as long as the test which is its second argument is false. The first argument is advanced upon the second argument being true.)

The sorting function really does work just like the tournament program for summing if we want to think of the merging operation as being like an indivisible operation. The sorting function then essentially works like mergesort, and is a linear algorithm, in both the best and worst case.

However, we *can* think of the merge operation as proceeding a bit at a time, working in parallel not just with merge operations at the same level (the same point in dimension t) but with merge operations at the other levels. When we do that, we see that, with enough processors, it is a linear algorithm in the worst case, and logarithmic in the best case. It is not clear how it behaves in the average case.

1.5 Summary

This chapter serves as an introduction to multidimensional declarative programming. We illustrated the basic concepts of this model of programming using several example programs including running sums, powers, sorting, and matrix multiplication. In particular, we show how multidimensional programming is naturally and serendipitously possible when an intensional point of view is adopted.

The example programs are written in the latest version of `Lucid`, which as before is declarative, and in its latest version offers powerful polydimensional capabilities including user-defined dimensions and dimensional abstraction.

Chapter 2

Intensionality

The intensional programming language, `Lucid`, described in Chapter 1 is based directly on intensional logic, a family of mathematical formal systems that permit expressions whose value depends on *hidden* contexts or indices. Our use of intensional logic is one in which the hidden contexts or indices are integers or tuples of integers. Intensional logic, as used to give semantics to natural language, uses a much more general notion of context or index.

Of course, intensional logic is hardly the first example of a formal system of interest to both logicians and computer scientists. The language `LISP` (invented by McCarthy and others in the early sixties [34]) was originally intended to be an adaptation of the lambda calculus, although it diverged in its treatment of variable-binding and higher-order functions. Shortly after, however, Landin produced `ISWIM`, the first true functional language [30].

These "logical" programming languages such as `ISWIM` are in many respects vastly superior to the more conventional ones. They are much simpler and better defined and yet at the same time more regular and more powerful. These languages are notationally closer to ordinary mathematics and are much more problem-oriented. Finally, programs are still expressions in a formal system, and are still subject to the rules of the formal system. It is therefore much easier to reason formally about their correctness, or to apply meaning-preserving transformations. With these languages, programming really is a respectable branch of applied mathematical logic.

These logic-based (or declarative) languages at first proved difficult to implement efficiently, and interest in declarative languages declined soon after the promising initial work of McCarthy and

Landin. Fortunately, the advent of large scale integration and new compiling technology reawakened interest in declarative languages, and brought about a series of new "second generation" declarative languages, such as `Prolog` [12] and `Miranda` [44].

`Lucid` itself was one of these second generation declarative languages. `Lucid` is based not so much on classical logical systems as on the possible worlds approach to *intensional logic*—itself a relatively new branch of logic [43] which reached maturity during the period (1965-75) in which declarative programming languages were in eclipse.

2.1 Intensional Logic

Intensional type of logic was originally developed to help understand natural languages, in which context sensitive expressions abound. For example, the phrase

five degrees less than yesterday's temperature

obviously denotes a numerical value. This value clearly depends on a numerical quantity called `temperature`. It also depends on the time of utterance, and on the place even though there is no explicit reference to either of these two parameters.

Stranger still is the manner in which the value of the expression depends on that of `temperature`. If we look outside and see that the thermometer reads (say) 35, we cannot conclude that the value referred to above is 30; in fact, we cannot conclude anything about the value, because the value of the expression on any given day depends on the value of temperature on the previous day.

In other words, the expression quoted seems to correspond to a mathematical expression of the form $y(t)-5$, where t is `temperature` and the function y corresponds to `yesterday's`. It is obvious, however, that there is no function y, from integers to integers, which makes the value of the mathematical expression corresponding to that of the cited phrase. The expression in question seems to violate the basic principle of *referential transparency*. (i.e., that the meaning of a whole expression depends only on the meaning of its parts).

For many years examples such as these were considered by logicians to be further evidence of the nonmathematical and illogical nature of natural languages. It was recognized that expressions like the one given could be translated into a "respectable" language like the predicate calculus, but only by introducing variables that refer explicitly to those factors (such as place and time) that implicitly determine the meaning of the natural language expression.

It is only comparatively recently that logicians discovered a more direct and natural way to capture formally these "context sensitive" operators and expressions. The solution to this long-standing puzzle is based on the distinction between what is called the *extension* and what is called the *intension* of expressions [43].

The *extension* of an expression is the value in a given context; for example, a truth value or (as with the example given above) an integer. A natural language expression can obviously have different extensions in different contexts. The *intension* gathers all these different extensions together, and captures the way in which the extensions depend on the contexts. In other words, the intension is the function that assigns to each context the value of the expression in that context.

The various paradoxes disappear once we realize that the intension is the true meaning of a natural language expression. Consider again the temperature example cited earlier. The intension of `temperature` is essentially a table giving the temperature on each day in question; part of the table might look like the following.

```
.. .. .. ..
30 Dec 84 23
31 Dec 84 21
 1 Jan 85 25
 2 Jan 85 23
 3 Jan 85 19
.. .. .. ..
```

The intension of **five degrees less than yesterday's temperature** is a similar table, part of which might look like the following.

```
.. .. .. ..
31 Dec 84 18
 1 Jan 85 16
 2 Jan 85 20
 3 Jan 85 18
 4 Jan 85 14
.. .. .. ..
```

It is now easy to see that the meaning of *five degrees ...* really does depend on the meaning of `temperature`, if we take the intensions to be these meanings. In fact we can obtain the intension of the former from that of the latter by the following method.

1. Subtracting 5 from all the temperatures in the right-hand column.

2. Advancing all the dates in the left hand column by one day.

We can even find a mathematically respectable function y that accurately captures the meaning of the phrase `yesterday's`. The function y, which maps intensions to intensions, simply increases all the dates by one day.

It is possible, of course, to formalize these ideas in a conventional, extensional logical system in which variables and expressions denote context-to-value functions. We could declare these objects to be the real extensions, thereby restore referential transparency, and dispose of the notion of intension. In practice, however, this approach is unnatural and impractical. Intensions are complicated mathematical objects. No one in their right mind would think of `temperature` as denoting some vast infinite table; nor would they consider statements about the temperature to be assertions about infinite tables. Furthermore, assertions involving a hidden context have a logic of their own which is in itself quite simple but which cannot be studied in a purely extensional system without ugly explicit context "indices."

Programmers very often think intensionally about programs in conventional language. For example, when examining the body of a procedure declaration, we cannot know exactly what values the procedure has—that depends on an implicit parameter, the "call" of the procedure in question. In the same way, the variables in the body can have many possible values-depending on another hidden parameter, namely the iteration index of the loop in question (and the indices of the enclosing loops).

We would not, however, characterize these languages as being *intensional.* They lack intensional operations—operations which, like `yesterday's`, give the programmer access to extensions in contexts other than the current one. In `Pascal`, for example, there is no operator that yields the value an expression had on the *previous* iteration. Nor is there an operator which, in a procedure body, gives the value an expression had in the "environment" from which the procedure was called.

By *Intensional Programming* we mean programming in a language that is also a formal system based on intensional semantics.

Intensional programmers should be encouraged to think intensionally (when appropriate), and should be provided with "context switching" operators which allow values from different contexts to be combined without explicit context manipulation.

2.2 The Intensional Language Lucid

Lucid was originally intended to be a purely declarative (nonprocedural) language in which iterative algorithms could be expressed easily and naturally. It was soon realized, however, that the language was well suited for expressing algorithms based on a dataflow view of computation—one in which data flows through a network of asynchronously operating processing stations [45].

The development of Lucid began in 1974, and at that time it was widely believed that declarative languages were inherently incapable of describing dynamic activity in any very natural way. The problem, so it seemed, was that logical languages dealt only with unchanging extensions, whereas iteration requires values that are constantly changing.

The paradox was resolved by basing the language on an intensional logic in which the values (extensions) of expressions and variables depend on an implicit natural number time parameter.

The original Lucid language [7] allowed only the (implicit) `time` dimension, and provided only the intensional operators `first`, `next`, `fby`, `asa`, `wvr`, and `upon`. Original Lucid was therefore a subset of the current version, provided we make the `time` dimension explicit for those operators.

Lucid otherwise looks very much like a functional programming language, and its `where` construct is copied almost directly from Landin's ISWIM. The inventors of Lucid were aware of the relationship between intensional logic and Lucid, through works such as [22].

The intensional interpretation of the special Lucid operators should be clear, given the examples presented in the introduction. The operator `next` takes us one moment ahead in time. The value of `next.time X` at a given point in time is the value `X` has at the next point in time. In the same way, `fby` takes us back one moment in time. The value of `A fby.time B` is the value `B` had on the previous instant-unless the time is 0, in which case the value of `A fby.time B` is the current (time 0) value of `A`.

Now consider the equation `i = 0 fby.time i+1`. Like all equations in a program, it is taken to be true at all points in time. This means that the value of `i` at any point in time is that of `0 fby.time i+1` at the same point in time. In other words, the value of `i` at any point in time is the value of `i+1` at the previous instant-or 0, if the time is currently 0. We can rephrase this as follows: `i` is initially 0, and the value at the next point in time is 1 plus the current value.

This way of looking at equations suggested a new implementation technique. Instead of trying to compile programs to imperative loop code, or dataflow nets, we compute the values of variables point by point. If we want, say, the value `i` at `time 3`, we consult the definition of `i` and conclude that the required value is the value of `i` at time 2, plus 1. In general, this gives a demand-driven scheme in which demands for the values at given times generate demands for other, possibly different, values at other, possibly different, times. This is the *eduction* model of computation, to be discussed in Chapter 5.

Equations defining functions, such as the definition

```
diff2(X) = next.time next.time X - 2 * next.time X + X
```

of the second difference operator `diff2`, are interpreted similarly. They are taken to be true for *all* values of the formal parameter(s) (in this case, all values of `X`) at *all* points in time. For example, it says that for any value of `X`, the value at time `5` of `diff2(X)` is the value of

```
next.time next.time X - 2 * next.time X + X
```

at time `5`.

The operational interpretations of the equations given in the introduction (in terms of iteration and coroutines, or streams and filters) are derived from the declarative, intensional reading.

2.3 Intensional versus Extensional Thinking

`Lucid` programmers can, if they choose, forget about intensional logic and consider `Lucid` programs to be ordinary extensional `ISWIM` programs in which the data objects are infinite sequences. In this view the operator `next`, given a sequence $<x_0, x_1, x_2, \ldots>$, returns the sequence $<x_1, x_2, x_3, \ldots>$. The operator `+` adds sequences componentwise. Even numerals like `1` denote infinite sequences (such as `<1,1,1, ...>`) whose components are all the same. This approach is mathematically correct and in fact the denotational semantics of Lucid is based on this formulation.

The extensional "infinite sequences" point of view is especially attractive to programmers who have experience with LISP and its successors, especially the lazy varieties (Miranda, Haskell, Scheme) which allow infinite lists. For many such people, the infinite sequence $<x_0, x_1, x_2, \ldots>$ corresponds exactly to the infinite list $[x_0, x_1, x_2, \ldots]$ and the Lucid operations **first**, **next** and **fby** correspond to the list operators **head**, **tail**, and **cons**.

From this purely extensional point of view the original (one dimensional) Lucid appears to be an idiosyncratic, severely restricted functional programming language. To begin with, early Lucid did not allow higher-order functions—a defect that, in the eyes of most functional programmers, is already fatal. Furthermore, they did not allow nested sequences-sequences of sequences. Although later versions (such as pLucid [19]) did support lists, they supported only finite lists, and distinguished between lists and sequences. Nor did it support lambda abstraction, user-defined types, pattern matching, or any of the other bells and whistles beloved of functional programmers.

In fact the only apparent advantage of Lucid over the Miranda family is the way in which entire sequences can be added pointwise, with the ordinary + operator. In the Miranda-style languages, the pointwise sum of two lists X and Y is denoted by a more elaborate expression, such as

```
{ x + y | x <- X, y <- Y }
```

Many functional programmers assumed that this apparently minor defect in Miranda-like languages could be remedied with a simple preprocessor.

Of course, some of the more glaring defects of early Lucid (such as the lack of higher-order functions) have been corrected. The important point, however, is that the comparison is fundamentally misguided. Lucid was never intended to be a traditional functional language, in which programs are typically higher order and involve recursive algorithms for manipulating hierarchically structured, possible infinite, data.

Instead, it was intended to be a more modest (but still declarative) language, in which programs typically involve iterative, possibly nonterminating algorithms over flat data structures, expressed in simple terms. In other words, Lucid was a much more modest, focussed language. The Miranda language is clearly more general, but generality is not the only measure of a programming system—as the experience with spreadsheets has demonstrated. In Miranda, even a simple running sum program involves explicit use of infinite lists and higher-order functions-concepts not inherent in the problem itself.

Thus the ability of the Lucid programmer to write A+B for the time-varying sum of two time-varying quantities is absolutely crucial, because it allows the programmer to think in terms of time-varying quantities, and so express a simple iterative algorithm in a simple form.

It is not easy to graft this feature on to existing functional languages. One problem, for example, is to decide which operations distribute pointwise, like +. Clearly not all operators distributed. For example, the list operations do not, otherwise they end up being applied to scalars. But if they don't distribute at all, you cannot write Lucid style iterative list algorithms. Then there is the problem of deciding which user-defined functions distribute, and by how much. Finally, the interaction between scalar-to-stream coercions and higher order-functions proves mind-boggling. No ad hoc scheme will ever replace the systematic application of intensional logic.

We should emphasize that the difference between Lucid and Miranda is more than notational, and the issues involved are deeper than programming methodology and mental hygiene. Lucid is implemented using eduction, whereas Miranda uses graph reduction. These computation models are very different, and although reduction is more general, eduction is simpler and has important advantages. (We discuss the essential differences in Chapter 5.)

2.4 Space and Time

Intensional reasoning arises naturally in many problems and usually involves contexts other than (or in addition to) time. Consider, for example, a classic problem in engineering: heat transfer in a solid. Suppose that we have a long thin metal rod that is initially cool (temperature 0) but whose left-hand end is in contact with a heat source (temperature 100). The heat will gradually diffuse through the rod, with parts nearer the heat source at first warming more quickly than those further away. The problem is to determine the temperature in various parts of the rod after a given interval.

We can compute an approximate solution to the problem by thinking of the rod as a sequence of small slices each of which at any point in time has a uniform temperature. We then apply the basic law of heat transfer, which says that the flow of heat between two bodies is proportional to the temperature difference. Let T_1 be the temperature of one of the slices (at some given point in time) and let T_0 and T_2 be the temperatures of the slices on the left and right, respectively (in general $T_0 \geq T_1 \geq T_2$). In any small interval of time the middle slice will gain an amount of heat proportional to $T_0 - T_1$, and lose an amount of heat proportional to $T_1 - T_2$. The new temperature of the middle slice will therefore be

$$(kT_0 - (1 - 2k)T_1 + kT_2)$$

for some small constant k depending on the length of the time interval and the properties of the metal.

Using this formula we can repeatedly "sweep" the rod and determine the heat distribution at successive time instants. In so doing, we are really using a simple discrete (central) difference approximation to solve the partial differential equation

$$\partial T/\partial t - a^2\partial^2 T/\partial s^2 = 0$$

(where a is a constant related to k).

This problem and the solution described involves an intension but one in which the extension (temperature again) now varies in *space* as well as in time. In other words, the context space is two dimensional: a particular context, which determines a particular temperature, consists of a time component and a space component.

Earlier extensions of `Lucid` [2, 20, 6] allowed intensions to vary in space as well as time. If we need only one dimension of space (as in the present example), it is enough to define our intensions as functions of two natural number parameters t and s.

Once we have the extra space dimension, we can solve the current problems with only two primitive spatial intensional operators, `right` and `sby` (pronounced *succeeded by*), which correspond more or less to `next` and `fby`. The value of `right X` at a given space point is the value of `X` at the space point immediately to the right. The value of `A sby B` at a given space point is the value of `B` at the space point immediately to the left if there is such a point; otherwise it is the value of `A` at the origin. More formally,

$$\texttt{right(F)}_t^s = \texttt{F}_t^{s+1}$$

$$\texttt{sby(F,G)}_t^s = \begin{cases} \texttt{F}_t^0 & (s = 0) \\ \texttt{G}_t^{s-1} & (s > 0) \end{cases}$$

The following equation formalizes the mathematical solution given above

```
T = 100 sby (0 fby.time (k*T - (1-2*k)*(right T) +
        k*(right right T));
```

Thus at any time t and space point s, $\texttt{T}_t^s$ is the temperature of slice s at time step t.

The heat transfer problem we just presented dealt only with an one-dimensional rod and was solved it by adding two primitive spatial intensional operators. In practice, problems of this nature usually involve at least two or three dimensions. To deal with these more general cases the language allows arbitrary numbers of space dimensions. This extended version of the language is called `Field Lucid` [20, 6] and an interpreter already exists for the language. The name `Field Lucid` was chosen because the language is well suited to problem solving over an n-dimensional space that changes with time.

Our next example is a solution to Laplace's equation using the usual *relaxation* method [23]. This program was originally written by Ashcroft [2] and we present it here in a slightly modified form. The relaxation method is well suited to the intensional paradigm as the value of a point in space is determined by the average value of its four immediate spatial neighbors at the previous point in time. The following is an outline of a program that solves Laplace's equation over a two dimensional space.

```
s where
   s = if ELECTRODE then POTENTIAL
                    else 0 fby.time avg(s) fi;
   avg(M) =(left M + right M + up M + down M)/4;
end
```

It defines variable `s` to, step by step, approach the potential field induced by various electrodes. For each point in the two-dimensional space (and independent of the step being considered), the variable `ELECTRODE` is `true` if the point lies within an electrode and the variable

`POTENTIAL` is the potential of the electrode at that point. The initial potential at all other points in the space is 0. This forms the basis for the relaxation method. At each step of the iteration, the value at a given space point outside the electrode becomes the average of the potentials of the four surrounding space points at the previous time instant. Successive approximations occur until the process settles down in some finite region of interest. (The above equation defines only the iterative process, without any provision for termination).

The definition of `avg` assumes that we have negative space coordinates. The intensional expression `left M` denotes the value of `M` at the current (horizontal) space coordinate minus one, just as `down M` denotes the value of `M` at the current vertical space coordinate minus one. `Field Lucid` does in fact support negative space and time coordinates. The negative space coordinates permits intensional programming using a full Euclidean space. The negative time coordinates are extremely useful for placing initial conditions used in the main computation (or main inductive definition). Without this these initial conditions would have to be placed in the first few points in time which is sometimes counter-intuitive. These additional features are defined by intensional operators that we have not defined in this book.

Note that this solution to Laplace's equation in 2-dimensions would work equally well in 3-dimensions by simply changing the definition of the average function to

```
avg(M) = (left M + right M + up M +
          down M + front M + rear M)/6;
```

where `front` and `rear` are similar to `left` and `right`, but in the third space dimension.

2.5 The Role of Extensional Thinking

In `Lucid`, programmers are (as we have already seen) more or less forced to think intensionally about time. In our experience, it is usually not a good idea to think of `Lucid` variables as giant immortal extensions. We therefore chose names such as `next` and `wvr` which strongly suggest an intensional interpretation.

`Field Lucid` was an intermediate language, lying between the original one-dimensional early `Lucid` and the current version. It provided an infinite set of predefined "space" dimensions in addition to the traditional time dimension. We have already seen examples in which spatial intensional thinking was natural and reflected the original problem statement. On the other hand, it seems that sometimes a "global", non-intensional view of space-varying entities is also appropriate.

Perhaps we should not be surprised that time and space differ in this fundamental way. After all, in the real world we are more or less forced to experience time moment-by-moment. Sometimes we experience space in the same way because we are immediately aware only of the local region of space which we are occupying: the room we are in, the street where we live, the city we are visiting. However, we are sometimes able to perceive whole regions of space at once: a floor plan of a building, a whole city seen from an airplane, a highway map of a state or province. We should therefore expect to be able to use both global and local (intensional) concepts in stating and solving problems involving space.

Unfortunately programmers found this rigorous distinction between time and space to be constricting and confusing, especially since the time dimension and the space dimensions were isomorphic. Furthermore, many problems clearly involved other dimensions, such as `employee` or `department` or `course` or indeed almost any set which can be used to index values that vary over the set. Why force the user to think of `course` as the vertical dimension and `student` as the horizontal dimension?

Also, problems arose concerning the relationships between the various space dimensions—are they all equal, or is the order significant (so that, for example, a matrix is really a vector of vectors)? In the end, when designing the latest `Lucid` we dropped any attempt to provide the user with a prepared set of ready-made dimensions, and instead allowed the user to declare and name their own problem-oriented dimensions to which they can attach their own interpretations.

2.6 Summary

Intensional programming means programming in a language or system based on intensional logic—the logic of expressions that vary according to implicit contexts or indices. In early `Lucid` the only context is discrete time. The successor language `Field Lucid` [6] supplied, in addition, a predefined set of "space" dimensions. The current language [17, 18] allows the user to instead declare and name their own dimensions, appropriate to the problem in question.

From a formal point of view, `Lucid` expressions denote functions from the context space to the data space. Thus `Lucid` can be considered a kind of functional programming. However, programming in Lucid is very different from programming in `Miranda` or `Haskell`, because in `Miranda` and `Haskell`, one is constantly reminded that expressions denote infinite objects. Traditional functional programming is clearly more general, but not generally more clear. Also, `Lucid` programs can be implemented using eduction, a form of demand-driven dataflow which has distinct advantages in comparison with graph reduction. This is discussed in Chapter 5.

Chapter 3

Syntax and Semantics

In this chapter, the syntax of `Lucid` will be formally specified. Also, the denotational semantics of `Lucid` will be outlined.

3.1 Syntax

The example programs in Chapter 1, surprisingly perhaps, informally introduced all the syntax of `Lucid`. There, we saw *where clauses*, *definitions*, *terms*, *dimension names variables*, *functions*, *constants*, and *operations*. Now, we will see how these syntactic entities are formalized, and the examples in the previous chapter will be looked at again, this time to see which of the syntactic entities are being used, and how.

`Lucid` is an expression-based language: every `Lucid` program is a *term*, which might be a where clause of size 1. A where clause of size n is an n-tuple of terms together with declarations of new dimensions and subsidiary definitions (that follow the keyword `where`). The definitions in a where clause have right-hand sides that may be where clauses. Thus, `Lucid` programs are naturally recursively structured, to arbitrary depth. We will say that `Lucid` is *where clause structured*, where we intend that expression to convey all that the expression *block structured* conveys about scoping in, say, `Algol`, `Pascal`, or `Ada`.

After that very cursory top-down view of `Lucid`, we now immediately look at the basic entities from which terms are formed: *variables*, *functions*, *constants*, and *operations*. These four basic types of entities we will call *atoms*.

Syntactically, variables and functions are represented by identifiers, which are alphanumeric strings that start with a letter. Constants and operations, on the other hand, are usually represented by characters other than letters, such as `+` and `3` and `#`. Some operations and constants *are* represented by alphanumeric strings, such as `fby`, `true`, and `div`. (Also, the ternary conditional operation is represented by four such strings: `if`, `then`, `else`, and `fi`.) We will say that these strings are not identifiers—they are special reserved keywords—and we will not allow them to be used to represent variables or functions. (This is standard practice for many languages.)

All atoms have two *arities*, which we will call the Roman and the Greek arities. The names "Roman" and "Greek" are used to allude to the Roman and Greek languages, not to any particular qualities of the Roman and Greek peoples. Greek arities, when they have a name, end in "adic", while Roman arities, when they have a name, end in "ary." For example, some small Roman arities are "unary," "binary," and "ternary." (These clearly are Roman-arity 1, Roman-arity 2, and Roman-arity 3, respectively.) Corresponding small Greek arities are "monadic," "dyadic," and "triadic."

The Roman arity indicates the number of arguments the atom takes, in the usual way. For example, we would say that a function is unary if it takes one argument, and that an operation is ternary if it takes three arguments. (The arguments of functions are called actual parameters, while the arguments of operations are called operands.)

The Greek arity indicates how many dimensions have to be focussed upon when the atom is used. For example, we would say that a variable is monadic if one dimension needs to be focussed upon, and that an operation is dyadic if two dimensions need to be focussed upon.

For an example that shows different arities, look at the definition of `runningSum` in Chapter 1. We see that the atom `runningSum` is a unary and monadic function, because it is defined to take one argument (indicated in the definition by a single formal parameter) and it requires the specification of one dimension to focus on (indicated in the definition by a single formal dimension). The atom `fby` is a binary, monadic operation and the atom `next` is a unary, monadic operation. The atom `+` is a binary, nulladic operation. (Note that a *nullary* atom takes no arguments and we use the invented terminology *nulladic* to describe an atom that needs no dimensions specified.) The atom `s` is a nullary, nulladic function.

Nullary functions are exactly the variables, and nullary operations are exactly the constants. (We therefore could have avoided introducing variables and constants as syntactic entities at all, but it doesn't seem worth the minor syntactic simplification of doing so. We will see that it is actually often very useful to be able to use the terms "variable" and "constant." In fact, because we are going use the terms "variable" and "constant", whenever we say "function" and "operation" it can be assumed that they are not nullary, unless we have explicitly said otherwise.

It should always be possible to determine the arities of an atom by inspection, as explained below.

Constants are always nullary, and are usually nulladic. (Examples are `3`, `true`, and `eod`.) The main example of a constant that is not nulladic is `#`; it is monadic. Basic operations like `+` and `if then else fi` are always nulladic. What used to be called the Lucid operations, such as `first`, `next`, `fby`, and `wvr`, are all monadic.

The arities of a variable or function can be determined by looking at the left-hand side of its definition, if it has one. (Every *function* that is used must have a definition, but some *variables* may not.) The number of formal parameters is the Roman arity and the number of formal dimensions is the Greek arity.

Every variable that is used but has no definition must be either a formal parameter or an input variable, and in both cases it will be nulladic.

Another basic syntactic entity that we need is that of *dimension names.* A dimension name will be an alphanumeric string. (If we want to, we can refer to dimensions `1`, `2`, and `3` as well as to dimensions `x`, `y`, and `z`.)

We are now ready to specify the syntax of `Lucid` programs.

3.1.1 Abstract Syntax

A *program* is a term.

A *term* is a where clause of size 1 or it is an atom, together with actual dimensions and arguments. In the latter case, if the atom has Greek-arity i and Roman-arity j, the term will have a length i sequence of distinct dimension names (the actual dimensions) and a length j sequence of terms (the arguments). The arguments are called *actual parameters* if the atom is a function (and the term itself is a *function call*), and they are called *operands* if the atom is an operation.

A *where clause of size n* is an n-tuple of terms, called the *subject* of the clause, a sequence of dimension names, and a set of definitions (of various sizes) of distinct variables and functions. The sequence of dimension names forms a *declaration*, a declaration that those dimensions are new and temporary. Together, the sequence of dimension names and the set of definitions form the *body* of the where clause.

A *definition of size n* consists of a left-hand side and a right-hand side. The *right-hand side* is simpler, so we will explain it first; it is simply a where clause of size n or, provided n is 1, a term. The *left-hand side* consists of an n-tuple of distinct functions or variables (which we will call the *siblings* of the definition if n is greater than 1), all with the same arities, both Greek and Roman (which we will call the Greek and Roman arities of the definition), and two sequences: a sequence of distinct dimension names (the *formal dimensions*) and a sequence of distinct nulladic variables (called the *formal parameters*). The lengths of the two sequences must match the Greek and Roman arities of the definition, respectively.

3.1.2 Concrete Syntax

A program is just a particular term.

When describing the concrete syntax for terms, we first will look at the simpler of the two cases, which is when the term in question is just an atom applied to other terms, focussed, perhaps, onto particular dimensions. The "other terms" are the arguments of the atom. If the atom is a function, it is written prefix (with parentheses), and if it is an operation it is written infix. The "particular dimensions" are the actual dimensions of the atom. This sequence of actual dimensions follows the atom, with a period between the two. (The period may be missing, of course, if there are no actual dimensions.)

The more complicated of the two cases for terms is when the term in question is a where clause of size 1.

In a where clause, the subject comes before the body. The body of a where clause begins with the keyword `where` and ends with the keyword `end`. The declarations in the body come before the definitions, and, since they are declaring new dimensions, they begin with the keyword `dimension`. They are terminated with semicolons.

The n-tuples of terms that are subjects of where clauses of size n, and the n-tuples of distinct variables in the left-hand sides of definitions of size n, will be enclosed in braces (unless n happens to be 1).

In definitions, the left-hand side and right-hand side are separated by =. They thus, deliberately, look like equations.

In function calls or in the left-hand sides of function definitions, the sequence of actual or formal dimensions comes before the sequence of actual or formal parameters. A useful mnemonic for this is "the Greeks came before the Romans." In a left-hand side that contains a sequence of formal dimensions, there is a period separating the n-tuple of variables or functions from the sequence of formal dimensions, unless that sequence is empty.

"Scope" Note: The functions and variables that are defined in the body of a where clause are "local" to that where clause; the definitions apply to both the subject and the body (but not outside). The same is also true of the new dimension names that are declared in the body. The formal dimensions and formal parameters used in the left-hand side of the definition of a variable or function can only be referred to in the right-hand side of the definition.

There is no automatic renaming of new dimensions to avoid clashes with existing dimensions, but users can always consistently rename new dimensions if they wish.

This has all been rather terse and formal. The best way to see that it really *is* describing the sorts of programs given so far is to look again at some of the programs in Chapter 1, and point out why they agree with the abstract and concrete syntax given above.

3.1.3 Running Sums Revisited

We have already looked at the definition of the function `runningSum` in order to identify the arities of the various atoms occurring in it.

3.1.4 Powers Revisited

The program given in Chapter 1 is

```
seq @.a (N - 1)
  where
    dimension a, b;
    seq = posint fby.a runningSum.b(drop.b(seq, n));
    posint = next.b #.b;
    runningSum.d(y) = s where
                            s = y fby.d next.d y + s;
                          end;
    drop.c(U, m) = U wvr.c wanted
```

```
                              where
                                wanted = (#.c + 1) mod m ne 0;
                              end;
        n = N fby.a n - 1;
     end
```

The program is a where clause of size 1, and the 1-tuple of terms that is its subject (no braces since n is 1) is

```
seq @.a (N - 1)
```

The atom of the term is the operation `@` and it has two operands, `seq` and `(N - 1)`, both of which are terms also. Notice how the term is written infix. The atom `@` has one actual dimension, namely `a`, which is attached to `@` by a period.

The body of the while statement has a length-2 sequence of dimension names (declaring the new dimensions `a` and `b`) and a length-5 sequence of definitions of size 1. The first, second, and fifth definitions define nulladic variables, namely `seq`, `posint`, and `n`. The third and fourth definitions define monadic functions, `runningSum`, which is unary, and `drop`, which is binary. The right-hand sides of the first, second, and fifth definitions are terms, whereas the third and fourth definitions are where clauses of size 1. They both have length-1 sequences of definitions, but both have empty sequences of dimension names-they don't declare any new dimensions.

The definition of `wanted`, inside the proper where clause defining the binary, monadic function `drop`, is the definition of a nulladic variable. Notice that it can not be focussed onto different dimensions but always tells us something about the position in dimension `c`. The dimension `c` itself will vary, however, because it is the formal dimension of the definition of `drop`. When `drop` gets focussed onto a particular dimension, `wanted` tells us something about that dimension, because that dimension will be the dimension `c` as far as `wanted` is concerned.

Notice that `N` is an input variable. It is crucial for the correct running of the program that `N` not vary in dimensions `a` or `b`, and since `a` and `b` are new dimensions, and therefore orthogonal to all others, the requirement is satisfied.

3.1.5 Matrix Multiplication Revisited

The matrix multiplication program from Chapter 1 is

```
sum.z(product,n)
  where
    dimension z;
    product = realign.y,z(A) * realign.x,z(B);
    realign.u,v(A) = A @.u #.v;
    sum.u(A, n) = B @.t (log n)
      where
        dimension t;
        B = A fby.t
            firstOfPair.u(A) + secondOfPair.u(A);
        firstOfPair.v(C) = C @.v (#.v * 2);
        secondOfPair.v(C) =  C @.v (#.v * 2 + 1);
      end;
  end
```

The program is a where clause of size 1, and the term that is the subject is simply a function call, focussed on dimension `z`. The function, `sum`, is defined in the body, of course. The formal dimension of `sum` is `u`. The right-hand side of the definition of `sum` is a where clause that declares and uses a new dimension `t`.

The definition of `sum` uses the variables `A` and `B`. These are not the same as the `A` and `B` used in the definition of `product`. One is a formal parameter and one is a local variable. The `A` and `B` in the definition of `product` are input variables.

The program has three input variables, in fact, the `A` and `B` used in the definition of `product` and the `n` used in the call of the function `sum`, on the first line of the program. There are also two *input dimensions*, `x` and `y`. These are dimensions that the user will be expected to know about, because he or she will be asked for the values of `A` and `B` at various points in dimensions `x` and `y`.

The input variable `n` must not vary in `x` or `y` if the matrix multiplication is to evaluate correctly. To ensure this, perhaps `n` should be replaced in line 1 by `first.x first.y n`. In fact, unless we do this, the user will be repeatedly asked for the value of `n` at different points in dimensions `x` and `y`, and, even if the answer is always the same, as is required, it will be a pain to the user to be repeatedly asked.

3.1.6 Sorting Revisited

The sorting function in Chapter 1 is as follows

```
sort.u(A, n) =
```

```
realign.w,u(B @.t (log n))
  where
    dimension t, w;
    B = (A fby.w eod) fby.t
        merge.w(firstOfPair.u(A), secondOfPair.u(A));
    firstOfPair.v(C) = C @.v (#.v * 2);
    secondOfPair.v(C) =  C @.v (#.v * 2 + 1);
    merge.a(x, y) =
      if iseod yy or xx <= yy then xx
                                else yy fi
      where
        xx = upon.a(x, iseod yy or xx <= yy);
        yy = upon.a(y, iseod xx or yy < xx);
      end;
    upon.a(x, p) =
      x @.a q
        where
          q = 0 fby.a if p then q + 1 else q fi;
        end;
  end;
```

(We have written upon as a function and given it a definition.) The sorting function takes the length-n list A in dimension u and returns it sorted in the same dimension. The right hand side of the definition of `sort` is a where clause of size 1 that has a body consisting of a declaration that dimensions `t` and `w` are new and a set of five definitions.

3.2 Denotational Semantics

The language Lucid has many novel and unusual features, such as intensionality, the use of arbitrary, even temporary, new dimensions, dimensionally abstracted definitions of variables and functions, and a serendipity principle that makes everything mean more than it appears at first sight. So what does this all really mean? What is its semantics?

The semantics of Lucid is denotational rather than operational. Rather than specify a conventional denotational semantics, we will indicate how the semantics has grown from the semantics of Lucid's predecessors, the earlier versions of Lucid described in Chapter 2 and the earlier functional languages.

The latest version of Lucid is a generalization of Field Lucid (fixed space and time dimensions), itself a generalization of original

Lucid (time only), which in turn was the result of adding temporal operators to ISWIM, Landin's generic functional language. We can therefore present the denotational semantics of Lucid in terms of a series of generalizations of the semantics of ISWIM.

All of these languages, ISWIM included, are really families of languages, each member determined by the choice of data objects and operations. The syntax of each family member is determined by the set of constants and operations symbols available, and the semantics is determined by an interpretation for these symbols. An interpretation in this sense consists of a domain D of data objects and a collection of operations (of appropriate arity) indexed by the set of operations symbols. These interpretations are just algebras; therefore every particular language is determined by the choice of the underlying data algebra. Given an algebra A, Lucid(A) is the member of the Lucid family based upon A.

Let us assume we have a chosen a fixed algebra A. In a sense, all the languages discussed are extensions of the simple expression language Exp(A). We begin by outlining the formal syntax and semantics of Exp(A).

Syntactically, Exp(A) "programs" are expressions built up from variables using the operation symbols in the signature of A (we will consider constants to be nullary operations). Thus, the meaning of an Exp(A) program is determined by the meanings of the variables; so we define an Exp(A) *interpretation* to be a function that assigns an element of D (the universe or data domain of A) to every variable.

Since Exp(A) has only two construction rules, the denotational semantics also has only two rules. The first rule says that the meaning of an expression consisting of a single variable is the value the given interpretation assigns to the variable. For example, the meaning of the expression X with respect to an interpretation I is I(X).

The second rule of Exp(A) semantics is that the meaning of an expression consisting of an operation symbol applied to operands is the result of applying the operation A associates with that symbol to the meanings of the operand expressions. For example, if D consists of the integers and A interprets the symbol + in the usual way, the basic rule implies that the meaning of a sum P+Q is the (numeric) sum of the meanings of P and Q.

The second language, ISWIM, extends *Exp* by adding function variables, **where** clauses, and recursive definitions (of both individual and function variables). Since there are two more construction rules, the denotational semantics has two more rules.

The first says that the meaning of an expression that consists of a function variable applied to actual parameters is the result of applying the meaning I associates with the function variable to the meanings of the actual parameters. For example, the meaning of `f(P,Q)` is the result of applying I(`f`) to the meanings of `P` and `Q`.

The second rule says that the meaning of a **`where`** clause is the meaning of the subject in the least interpretation I' that (1) makes all the definitions in the body true and (2) differs from I at most in the values assigned to the local variables of the **`where`** clause (those variables with definitions in the clause). Here the definitions are considered as *literally* being equations—an interpretation satisfies a definition if and only if both sides have the same meaning, for all values of the formal parameters.

Of all those interpretations that make the definitions true (there may be more than one) we select the one that is *least* in the domain-theoretic sense. Roughly speaking, this is the solution that can be calculated by using the definitions as computation rules. (This *least fixpoint* semantics is described in more detail in [45]). For least fixpoints to be defined, the original algebra A has to be a continuous algebra, which implies that its universe must be a complete partial order with a least element $\perp$ ("bottom").

The original (temporal) Lucid extends ISWIM by adding the temporal operators **`first`**, **`next`** and **`fby`** and by reinterpreting expressions as time sequences. Functions and operations map sequences to sequences, with the operations of A reinterpreted as acting pointwise on sequences.

More formally, the algebra $Lu(A)$ assigns to each variable an element of D^N, N the set of natural numbers.

The only new rules we need are the familiar rules for the `Lucid` operators. For example, the rule for **`next`** says that the meaning of **`next`** `P` is $\lambda t \;\; \pi(t+1)$, where π is the meaning of `P`. Another way of stating this rule, more in the spirit of intensionality, is to say that the value of **`next`** `P` at time t is that of `P` at time $t+1$.

The rule about the interpretations of the operations of A must be altered to reflect the fact that these now work pointwise on intensions. For example, the modified rule implies that the value of `P+Q` at time t is the sum of the value of `P` at time t and the value of `Q` at time t.

The other rules for ISWIM carry over *unchanged* to temporal Lucid (we are omitting the old **is current** construct, whose semantics entailed a departure from that of the ISWIM **where** clause).

Field Lucid and similar extensions added space as well as time dimensions. These languages were still dimensionally static in the sense that have a fixed, predefined set K of dimensions and a corresponding fixed collection of operations over these dimensions.

In each of these dimensions a coordinate is still a natural number; the context space is therefore N^K, the set of all K-indexed families of natural numbers. Since an intension is a map from the context space to the data domain; the space of intensions is therefore D^{N^K}.

Data operations still work pointwise, so that the value of P+Q at coordinate c is the sum of the value of P at coordinate c and the value of Q at coordinate c.

The temporal operations like **next** have to be reinterpreted to map D^{N^K} to itself. In fact most of the intensional operations affect only a few dimensions but have to formally map the entire intension space to itself. We do this by making them work pointwise on the other dimensions. For example, the **realign** operation is naturally defined on to space dimensions (say **row** and **column**). If there is also a **time** dimension, we treat a three-dimensional intensions as a **time** stream of matrices, and we apply the **realign** operation *pointwise* to every element of the stream.

The other semantic rules are still unchanged.

Finally, we can consider the semantics of Lucid itself. The crucial difference is that there is no longer a predefined set of dimensions over which everything varies. We can assume the existence of a *large* set Δ of *possible* dimensions, but we cannot simply treat every variable as denoting an element of D^{N^Δ}. The problem is that **where** clauses involve "fresh" dimensions that are not already in use.

The correct way is to consider a variable as denoting a whole family of normal intensions, but of arbitrarily large dimensionality. For example, suppose that X is *really* a **row-column** array, and therefore *really* an element of D^{L^N} with N = {**row**,**column**}. We can *inflate* X into a {**row**,**column**,**time**} intension by making it constant in time. In other words, any L-dimensional intension can be inflated into a K-dimensional intension (K a superset of L) by making the inflated version constant over the dimensions in K-L. The semantics of Lucid is based on treating the inflated version as another representative of the same entity, formally speaking, meanings are equivalence classes.

Now suppose that one representative of the meaning of `P` is a $K1$ dimensional intension X, and that one representative of the meaning of `Q` is a $K2$ dimensional intension Y. To construct a representative of the meaning of `P+Q`, we inflate X and Y into $K1 \cup K2$-dimensional intensions X' and Y', then add them pointwise. Of course we have to prove that this process is insensitive to the original choice of representatives-that different choices for X and Y result in something equivalent to the first result.

Next, suppose that `X` is a K-dimensional representative of the meaning of `P`. To construct the meaning of **`next`** `X` we inflate X to a $K \cup \{$`time`$\}$-dimensional intensions X' then apply inflated version of **`next`** to it.

Finally, we must modify the `ISWIM` semantics of **`where`** to take declared dimensions into account. First we choose particular representatives of all the global variables of the **`where`** clause. Suppose that `d` and `e` are the new dimensions declared in the clause. We choose two arbitrary elements d and e in Δ that do *not* appear in any the dimensionality of any of these global representatives. Then we construct the least fixed point of the body and evaluate the subject, yielding a representative S of dimensionality K. The last step is to *deflate* S to dimensionality $K - \{d, e\}$, and we do this by setting the dimension `d` and `e` components to 0.

The remaining definitions (importantly, function application) remain unchanged. In particular, dimensionally abstract functions pose no particular problem—we can treat "dimension" as a separate type.

As the reader may suspect, we have glossed over some nontrivial mathematical subtleties, but the basic concepts should be clear. For example, we have to show that at every stage the we are dealing with finite dimensional entities—that almost all the representatives of the meaning of an expressions are inflations of a finite dimensional intension (and we need a similar result for functions). This finiteness result ensures us that as long as Δ is infinite, we will always have "fresh" dimensions available.

3.3 Summary

In this chapter, the abstract and concrete syntax of the latest version of `Lucid` has been given. The examples described informally in Chapter 1 including running sums, powers, matrix multiplication, and sorting have been reconsidered from a formal syntactic viewpoint. Also the denotational semantics to the language has been outlined by viewing the language as a series of generalizations of Landin's `ISWIM`.

Chapter 4

Transformation and Verification

The ability to verify and reason about programs was one of the main goals behind the design and development of `Lucid`. In fact, from its very inception `Lucid` was intended to be not just a programming language, but also a formal system in which program specifications and correctness proofs could be expressed as well. Our goal was a formal programming system in which programs for "realistically" complicated problems could be proved correct with only a realistic amount of effort.

4.1 Simple Introductory Example

The nonprocedural nature of `Lucid` and its mathematical semantics led naturally to a reasoning technique where properties proved of variables and functions (assertions) are true throughout the where clauses in which the variables and functions are defined, and are not just thought of as being true at particular points where they are "attached" (as would be the case in the usual verification technique for procedural programs). In that respect, `Lucid` verification is like verification of functional programs. The assertions proved for `Lucid`, however, have the basic simplicity of the assertions proved in the procedural case, and the proofs are very similar.

We will illustrate the differences by using a very simple program for computing integer square roots. We will express it in an imperative language, in a functional language, and in `Lucid` and show how verification would be performed for each language using the different techniques. In all three techniques, we will use the following terminology from the procedural approach, namely that the *precondition* is a restriction on the inputs of a program and the *postcondition* is a desired property of the outputs of the program, assuming that the inputs satisfied the precondition.

A simple Pascal-like program for computing the integer square root of a non-negative integer n might be

```
program(input, output);
   var x, y : integer;
  begin
   x := 1; y:= 1;
   readln(n);
   while x <= n do
      begin
         x := x + 2*y + 1;
         y := y + 1;
      end;
   writeln(y - 1)
  end.
```

To prove that this program is correct, that is, for precondition $N \geq 0$, it satisfies the postcondition

$$Y \times Y \leq N < (Y + 1) \times (Y + 1)$$

where Y is the value written out for input N, one attaches to the program the assertion

$$(y - 1) \times (y - 1) \leq n \ \& \ x = y \times y$$

just before the test in the while statement. Provided that the precondition $N \geq 0$ is true, that is, the input is non-negative, the assertion will be *valid*, that is, it will be true whenever control reaches the point where the assertion is attached. It will not necessarily be true at other points. In particular, it will probably be *false* between the two assignments, to x and y, inside the while loop.

This establishes partial correctness: if the precondition is initially true then the program terminates the final values of Y and N satisfy the postcondition.

A Lucid program to do the same thing would be

```
(y - 1) asa.a x > n
   where
```

```
        dimension a;
        x = 1 fby.a x + 2*y + 1;
        y = 1 fby.a y + 1;
    end
```

(This essentially is the first Lucid program that was ever written, back in 1974, and it was written in order to then investigate its verification.)

To prove that this program is correct (i.e., that it satisfies the same postcondition)

$$\mathtt{Y} \times \mathtt{Y} \leq \mathtt{N} < (\mathtt{Y} + 1) \times (\mathtt{Y} + 1)$$

where Y is the scalar (i.e., dimensionless) value of the whole program and N is the scalar value of the input variable n (i.e., the value that is inputted) one first proves the assertion

$$\mathtt{x} = \mathtt{y} \times \mathtt{y}$$

about the local variables of the where clause. This assertion is then true wherever those variables can be referred to (i.e., throughout the where clause). That means that it is true for every context for that where clause, which means at every point in dimension a. Thinking iteratively, the points in dimension a correspond to stages in the computation of the values of x and y. The assertion is therefore an invariant (i.e., something true at every stage of the computation of the where clause).

Beside this invariant assertion, we also need to prove that

$$(\mathtt{y} - 1) \times (\mathtt{y} - 1) \leq \mathtt{n}$$

at the point when, or where, x first exceeds n. This sounds like an assertion attached at a particular point in the program, but, in fact, what we actually prove is

$$(\mathtt{y} - 1) \times (\mathtt{y} - 1) \leq \mathtt{n} \ \mathtt{asa} \ \mathtt{x} > \mathtt{n}$$

(This involves showing that the point at which x first exceeds n actually exists.) Moreover, in order to prove that

$$(\mathtt{y} - 1) \times (\mathtt{y} - 1) \leq \mathtt{n}$$

at that point, the precondition $\mathtt{N} \geq 0$ will be used. We then have that

$$(\mathtt{y} - 1) \times (\mathtt{y} - 1) \leq \mathtt{n} < (\mathtt{y} - 1 + 1) \times (\mathtt{y} - 1 + 1) \quad \mathtt{asa} \ \mathtt{x} > \mathtt{n}$$

and we can push the asa through its left hand argument, giving

$$((\texttt{y} - 1) \ \texttt{asa} \ \texttt{x} > \texttt{n}) \times ((\texttt{y} - 1) \ \texttt{asa} \ \texttt{x} > \texttt{n})$$
$$\leq \texttt{n} <$$
$$(((\texttt{y} - 1) \ \texttt{asa} \ \texttt{x} > \texttt{n}) + 1) \times (((\texttt{y} - 1) \ \texttt{asa} \ \texttt{x} > \texttt{n}) + 1)$$

Finally, noting that

$$(\texttt{y} - 1) \ \texttt{asa} \ \texttt{x} > \texttt{n}$$

is the value Y of the whole program and that N is the value of the input variable n, we get the postcondition

$$\texttt{Y} \times \texttt{Y} \leq \texttt{N} < (\texttt{Y} + 1) \times (\texttt{Y} + 1)$$

Note that the proof for the Lucid program is somewhat similar to the proof for the Pascal-like program, but it establishes total correctness and not just partial correctness. Moreover, the technique is different in that properties are not established about particular points in the program but about whole regions (in this case, the region within the where clause).

In this latter respect, the technique for Lucid is similar to the partial correctness technique for functional programs, as we will now illustrate for the functional program for the same integer square roots problem

```
iSqRoot(n) = f(n, 1, 1)
f(n, x, y) = if x > n then y - 1
                       else f(n, x + 2*y + 1, y + 1)
```

The technique entails finding assertions AiSqRoot(n, z) and Af(n, x, y, z) that are valid such that

- (a) AiSqRoot(n, iSqRoot(n)) is true if iSqRoot(n) is defined, and
- (b) Af(n, x, y, f(n, x, y)) is true if f(n, x, y is defined.

The assertions should be strong enough to establish the postcondition, given the precondition. That is,

$$\texttt{N} \geq 0 \ \& \ \texttt{AiSqRoot(N, Y)} \Rightarrow \texttt{Y} \times \texttt{Y} \leq \texttt{N} < (\texttt{Y} + 1) \times (\texttt{Y} + 1)$$

must be true.

In order to establish (a) and (b), the technique requires that the following be true:

$$\texttt{Af(n, 1, 1, z)} \Rightarrow \texttt{AiSqRoot(n, z)}$$

$$\texttt{x > n} \Rightarrow \texttt{Af(n, x, y, y - 1)}$$

$$\texttt{x} \leq \texttt{n} \ \& \ \texttt{Af(n, x + 2*y + 1, y + 1, z)} \Rightarrow \texttt{Af(n, x, y, z)}$$

The following assertions satisfy the conditions:

$$\begin{array}{lcl} \texttt{AiSqRoot(n, z)} & \Leftrightarrow & \texttt{z} \times \texttt{z} \leq \texttt{n < (z + 1)} \times \texttt{(z + 1)} \\ \texttt{Af(n, x, y, z)} & \Leftrightarrow & \texttt{x} = \texttt{y} \times \texttt{y} \ \& \ \texttt{(y - 1)} \times \texttt{(y - 1)} \leq \texttt{n} \\ & \Rightarrow & \texttt{z} \times \texttt{z} \leq \texttt{n < (z + 1)} \times \texttt{(z + 1)} \end{array}$$

It can be seen from this example that the Lucid verification technique is similar to the functional programming verification technique in that the assertions used describe the values computed rather than those attached to particular points in the program. It is also similar to the procedural programming verification technique, in that the assertions involved, and the proofs required, are very similar in the procedural and Lucid cases.

In the above example no details were given of the basic manipulations or transformations of logical formulae that were involved, because they were very similar in all three cases. Nevertheless, there are differences in technique.

In the Lucid technique, the formulae are not attached to points in the program but are associated with the where clauses in which the variables involved are "in scope." We shall say that the formulae *annotate* the where clause, and form an *annotation.* Within the annotation we can make changes by logical deduction. Within the program we can make changes by program transformation. Since the definitions in a where clause are actually equations, it is not surprising that they can be copied from the program to the annotation. We will see that it is also possible to copy formulae from the annotation to the program, that is, we can perform transformations of a program as a result of properties of the program that we have proved. Program verification and transformation go together.

In this chapter we will continue by first considering transformation. A lot of what we will say is based upon the chapter entitled Program Transformation in [45], modified to take into account subsequent changes and extensions to the language.

4.2 Program Transformation

A program transformation is a rule that allows one to make changes in a program (usually, small changes) that preserve the *meaning* of the program. The "meaning" of a program is the role it performs when considered as a "black box." It is the transformation that the program applies to its input. In other words, the meaning of a program is its *input-output function.* If T is a program to which a transformation is to be applied, and T' is the modified program which results, then and T' produce the same output when given the same input. The two programs are said to be *equivalent.* Of course, by "the same input" we mean the same responses to requests for values of the same variables in the same contexts. Equivalent programs are, as "black box" filters, interchangeable. It is possible, of course, that equivalent programs may *perform* differently-one may do its work more quickly than the other, the other might use more resources than the first—but, as far as end results are concerned, the programs are (from the "outside") indistinguishable.

Every programmer uses the notion of input/output equivalence, at least informally. Programs are continually being modified, often solely to improve their performance. Any modifications to a working program would be expected not to alter the results; the modifications should be equivalence-preserving transformations. Often, programmers will write code that they know is inefficient and expect to spend some time later improving its performance. Initially it is most important to rapidly get a program that is simple and obviously correct. Once the "quick and dirty" version is running, it can be gradually transformed into a more efficient but still equivalent program. The strategy is a common and effective one and is used in "rapid prototyping," where its existence is essential for rapid prototyping's effectiveness.

Most imperative programmers use only a very informal approach to the problem of program modification. There are a few precise transformation rules that can be applied (for example, renaming the dummy parameters of a procedure definition) but they are very rare. The existence of side effects, pointers, and aliasing (among other things) make it very difficult to isolate the effects of even a very small change. For example, in `Pascal` we cannot in general replace the integer expression

```
i+m(8)
```

by

```
m(8)+i
```

because the function `m` may affect the value of `i`. Nor can we reverse the order of the two apparently unrelated commands

```
x := a;
y := b;
```

because `x` may be another name for `b`.

In Lucid, however (as in ISWIM and most nonprocedural languages) the situation is much different. There are no side effects, pointers, or aliasing. The expressions

```
i+m(8)
```

and

```
m(8)+i
```

always yield the same value, and any two definitions in the body of a clause may be interchanged. The reason, of course, is that Lucid is based on the notation of ordinary mathematics, the arithmetic and other data operations are referentially transparent, and the statements in a clause really are equations. In Lucid it is possible to formulate a number of reasonably simple yet extremely powerful transformation rules that take advantage of the situation. The rules allow us (for example) to perform symbolic calculations on data, expand function calls, eliminate unnecessary definitions, and even collapse whole clauses to a single expression. These rules are even powerful enough to allow us to symbolically "evaluate" entire programs by transforming them to expressions consisting of a single constant. Most of these rules have their origins in the reduction rules of the Lambda Calculus. Darlington and Burstall used similar rules as the basis of their program transformation system [14], and others have extended this work.

The transformation rules are especially effective when used in conjunction with induction principles (one example of which will be given in a later section). They make it possible to transform one program into a totally different one that computes its results by a completely different method.

One especially attractive feature of transformation rules in general is that they require no knowledge of any formal system other than the programming language itself. There is no need for the programmer to learn a second, more complicated assertional "metalanguage" for stating properties of programs. Some of the rules require carefully stated restrictions concerning the scope of variables, but scope is something a programmer must understand anyway.

4.2.1 The Basis Rule

We begin by considering the following simple program

```
2+2
```

to add two and two. There is, of course, an even simpler program to which the above is equivalent, namely the program

```
4
```

It ought to be possible to transform the first into the second. The rule that allows us to carry out this transformation is the *Basis Rule.* The Basis Rule is essentially "substitution of equals for equals," where the equality in question comes from mathematics or from properties of operators in `Lucid`, not from the structure of the program in question.

The statement of the Basis Rule is as follows: If A is a continuous algebra, `T` is a `Lucid(`A`)` program, and `R = L` is an equation true in *Lu(A)* (in the sense of ordinary equational algebra), then any occurrence of `R` in `T` can be replaced by `L`.

P is a continuous algebra of objects and operations found in the language `POP-2` [9]. Since the equation `2+2=4` is true in *Lu(P)*, we are allowed to transform the `pLucid` (i.e., `Lucid(`P`)`) program `2+2` into the pLucid program `4`.

The equation referred to in the Basis Rule may involve terms with occurrences of variables and functions and dimension names. Such an equation is true in an algebra if and only if (and this is the convention of universal algebra) the two sides have the same value for all values of the variables and functions in question and no matter what dimensions we are talking about. For example, since the equation

```
f.a(x-1)*x = x*f.a(x-1)
```

is true in *Lu(P)*, the Basis Rule allows us to transform the program

```
f.t(i) asa.t i eq n
 where
   dimension t;
   i = 1 fby.t i+1;
   f.a(x) = 1 fby.t f.a(x-1)*x;
 end
```

into the program

```
f.t(i) asa i eq n
 where
   dimension t;
   i = 1 fby.t i+1;
   f.a(x) = 1 fby.t x*f.a(x-1);
 end
```

In the same way the equations

```
if true then x else y fi = x
if false then x else y fi = y
```

can be used to "evaluate" boolean expressions.

The question which immediately arises, of course, is how do we know that a given equation is true in *Lu(P)*? There are a small number of important equations such as

```
first.t(x fby.t y) = first.t x
next.t(x fby.t y) = y
first.t x fby.t next.t x = x
next.t(x+y) = next.t x + next.t y
next.s next.t x = next.t next.s x
(A @.x i) @.y j = (A @.y j) @.x i
(provided x and y are different)
(y @.t #.s) @.s i = y @.t i
(provided y does not vary in dimension s)
```

that are true in *Lu(A)* for all *A*. These can be verified "in the metalanguage", by directly referring to the definition of *Lu(A)*.

The truth of a much larger collection of equations follows from the Extension Principle: if an equation has no occurrences of Lucid operators (i.e., no occurrences of polyadic operators) and is true in *A*, then it is also true in *Lu(A)*.

The Principle still leaves us with the problem of discovering equations true in *A*. This last problem, however, has nothing to do with Lucid or with programming per se; the question is rather one of formal reasoning about data types. We will not discuss this subject here except to point out that equations true in A could be derived from an equational specification of A.

There is also an important generalization of the Extension Principle that gives us many useful equations. The Generalized Extension Principle guarantees the truth of any equation obtained (without name clashes) from an equation true in *Lu(A)* by uniformly substituting arbitrary terms for free occurrences of nulladic variables. This statement refers to two concepts, namely those of "free occurrence" and "name clash", that need to be explained.

A free occurrence of a nulladic variable in a term is one that is not in the left-hand side of a definition in a where clause, is not in the right-hand side of a definition in a where clause that has the variable as one of the locals of the where clause, and also is not in the right-hand side of a definition that has the occurrence as one of its formal parameters.

A free occurrence of a dimension name in a term is one which is not in a declaration in a where clause, and also is not in the lefthand side of a definition in a where clause, and also is not in the righthand side of a definition in a where clause which has a declaration of the dimension name, and also is not in the righthand side of a definition which has the occurrence as one of its formal dimensions.

In other words, a free occurrence is one where the variable or dimension has its "outer" meaning. For example, in the term

```
f(next.c x + Y)
 where
   dimension c;
   Y = y - 1;
   a = realign.t,c(A);
   b = realign.t,c(B);
   realign.a,b(C) = C @.a #.b;
   s.d = f.d(Y upon.d x>0)
        where
         f.c(a) = a*x + next.c b;
        end;
   x = a*w - s.c;
   w = a/b
        where
         b = 5+x;
         x = 5;
        end;
 end
```

the occurrences of a on the line

```
f.c(a) = a*x + next.c b;
```

are not free (i.e., they are *bound*) because here a is being used as a formal parameter. The other five occurrences of a in the program are not free because they are referring to a local of the outer where clause or a formal dimension of a definition. The first of the five is the lefthand side of a definition, the second and third are formal dimensions in a definition, while the other two are within righthand sides of definitions.

The occurrence of b on the line just cited is not free because it is a local of the outer where clause, and its occurrence later, in the expression

```
a/b
```

is not free because b is a local of the clause of which this expression is the subject.

In the expression

```
f(next.c x + Y)
```

which is the subject of the main clause, the occurrences of x, Y, and c are not free. Both of the variables are locals; they are defined in the body. Dimension c is local; it is declared in the body. (In fact, for the same reason, none of the occurrences of dimension name c in the where clause are free.

The occurrences of d in the line

```
s.d = f.d(Y upon.d x>0)
```

are bound because d is the formal dimension of this definition of s. The two occurrences, in the outer definitions of a and b, of the dimension t are free. Finally, the occurrence of the variable y in

```
Y = y - 1;
```

is free. The free variables and dimensions of this term are therefore A, B, y, and t.

When an occurrence of a nulladic variable or a dimension name is free, it has its "outer" meaning. If we are going to replace it by a term or another dimension name, they, too, should have their outer meanings as well. However, sometimes substitutions will be made into contexts in which some of the free nulladic variable or dimension names become bound. In this situation we say that there is a *clash* of variables or dimensions. There will then be a confusion between two different meanings of the same symbol.

Having explained the concepts of free occurrence and name clash, we will now continue by illustrating, by examples, the Generalized Extension Principle.

The equation

```
p + q = q + p
```

using nulladic variables `p` and `q` is true in `Lu(P)` (because it is true in `P`). By substituting the term `x` for `p`, and the term `f.a(x-1)` for `q`, we obtain the equation

```
x*f.a(x-1) = f.a(x-1)*x
```

Of course, we have already claimed that this equation is true in *Lu(A)*, but the Generalized Extension Principle shows that depends on a much simpler equation true in A, followed by substitution of terms for nulladic variables.

Unfortunately, there is one serious limitation to the use of the Basis Rule: the equations true in the underlying algebra are not always those expected. For example, consider the *Lucid(Z)* program

```
f(i)
  where
   f(x) = f(x) - f(x);
  end
```

with Z being a continuous algebra based on the integers. We might be tempted to use the "obviously" true equation

```
p - p = 0
```

derive

```
f(x) - f(x) = 0
```

and transform our program to

```
f(i)
 where
  f(x) = 0;
 end
```

which outputs 0's, no matter what `i` is. The transformation is incorrect; the original program does not output anything at all. The flaw in the reasoning is in assuming the correctness of the equation

```
p - p = 0
```

This equation is *not* true in Z, because it fails when p has the value $\perp$. In general, the presence of the extra partial objects in a continuous algebra can invalidate many supposedly natural equations (especially those involving two or more occurrences of the same variable on one side).

4.2.2 The Calling Rule

The Basis Rule discussed earlier is based on the principle that expressions in Lucid are referentially transparent; it says that expressions having the same value can be interchanged. The Calling Rule is also based on this principle, and on the fact that the statements in a where clause really are equations. The Calling Rule says that (roughly speaking) occurrences of a variable or function, together with actual dimensions and actual parameters, can be replaced by the relevant definition. (The formal statement of the rule will be given later after first giving a few examples of its use.)

Consider, for example, the following simple program

```
x.a + y.a where x.r = #.r; y.s = #.s; end
```

using a where clause. The subject of the where clause is the expression `x.a + y.a` but it is obvious that in this context both `x.a` and `y.a` have the value `#.a`. Thus we would expect that the program above is equivalent to

```
#.a + #.a where x.r = #.r; y.s = #.s; end
```

(Our later rules will allow us to convert this in turn to `#.a + #.a` and, subsequently, `2 * #.a`).

To formalize all this, we first need to be aware of the conditions (discussed earlier) under which we are able to substitute terms for nulladic variables and substitute new dimension names for dimension names.

The body of the example term above contains the definition

```
x = a*w - s.c;
```

We can therefore use the Calling Rule to replace relevant occurrences of `x` by `a*w - s.c`. One relevant occurrence is that in the subject of the main clause. If we perform the substitution, the result is

```
f(next.c(a*w - s.c) + Y)
 where
   dimension c;
   Y = y - 1;
   a = realign.t,c(A);
   b = realign.t,c(B);
   realign.a,b(C) = C @.s #.b;
   s.d = f.d(y upon.d x>0)
         where
          f.c(a) = a*x + next.c b;
         end;
   x = a*w - s.c;
   w = a/b
         where
          b = 5+x;
          x = 5;
         end;
 end
```

None of the variables and dimensions in

```
a*w - s.c
```

are bound in the new context any differently than they were in the definition of `x`, and no clash of variables results. This substitution is allowed.

The Calling Rule would also allow us to substitute for the second relevant occurrence of `x`, in the expression

```
f.d(y upon.d x>0)
```

There is one more relevant occurrence of `x`, namely that in the definition

```
f.c(a) = a*x + next.c b,
```

but the Calling Rule does not allow the substitution to be performed, for two reasons. The first problem is that a name clash involving the variable `a` results. The second problem is that the dimension `c` in the definition is a formal dimension. If we ignored the restrictions and substituted anyway, the result would be the definition

```
f.c(a) = a*(a*w - s) + next.c b;
```

This new definition, however, has a different meaning from the old one. The second occurrence of `a` in the right hand side of the definition now refers to the argument of `f`, and not the “outer” value of `a`.

Also, the dimension c in the right hand side is a dummy dimension, and is not related to the outer c. There is no reason to expect that the transformed term will have the same meaning as the original.

There is, of course, one more occurrence of x in a subexpression, namely that in the definition

```
b = 5 + x;
```

but this occurrence is not relevant to the definition

```
x = a*w - s.c;.
```

It occurs inside a clause whose body contains a different definition of x (namely `x = 5;`) and innermost definitions always take precedence. We could, however, use the Calling Rule with this inner, relevant definition and replace the occurrence of x by 5. The resulting term would be

```
f(next.c(a*w - s.c) + Y)
 where
   dimension c;
   a = realign.t,c(A);
   b = realign.t,c(B);
   realign.a,b(C) = C @.a #.b;
   Y = y - 1;
   s.d = f.d(Y upon.d x>0)
        where
         f.c(a) = a*x + next.c b;
        end;
   x = a*w - s.c;
   w = a/b
        where
         b = 5+5;
         x = 5;
        end;
 end
```

We will now consider examples of the Calling Rule applied to *function* definitions. Consider, for example, the very simple program

```
sum(2,3)
 where
  sum(x,y) = x + y;
 end;
```

It seems perfectly obvious that the definition of sum implies that the expression sum(2,3) has the same value as 2 + 3. We would reason as follows: the first argument of `sum`, which is called `x` in the definition, is "actually" `2`, and the second argument, which is called `y`, is "actually" `3`. The value of `sum(2,3)` should therefore be that of the expression `x + y` when `2` is substituted for `x` and `3` is substituted for `y`.

We will now *formalize* the Calling Rule:

Let W be a clause containing a definition of size k of the form

$$\{F_1, F_2, .., F_k\}.a_0, a_1, .., a_{m-1}(P_0, P_1, ..., P_{n-1}) = E;\}$$

where the F's are functions (variables if n is 0), the a_i's are formal dimensions, the P_j's are formal parameters, and E is a where clause of size k (or, if $k = 1$, a term).

Then any relevant occurrence in the clause of a term of the form

$$F_d.b_0, b_1, ..b_{m-1}(A_0, A_1, .., A_{n-1})$$

can be replaced by a term E' in the following way. We first find the term E_d defining F_d. (If k is greater than 1, this involves constructing a where clause of size 1 from E using the same body as E but only one, the d-th, subject term. If $k = 1$, then E_d is E.) Now E' is the result of substituting (simultaneously) b_0 for all free occurrences of a_0 in E_d, b_1 for all free occurrences of a_1 in E_d, .., b_{m-1} for all free occurrences of a_{m-1} in E_d, A_0 for all free occurrences of P_0 in E_d, A_1 for all free occurrences of P_1 in E_d, .., and A_{n-1} for all free occurrences of P_{n-1} in E_d. As before, these substitutions and the final replacement must not give rise to any clashes of variables.

An expression of the form $F_d.b_0, b_1, ..b_{m-1}(A_0, A_1, .., A_{n-1})$ can be thought of as a "call" of the function F_d (hence the name of the rule) with actual dimensions $b_0, b_1, .., b_{m-1}$, and actual parameters $A_0, A_1, .., A_{n-1}$. The rule says that such a "call" to F_d can be replaced by the "body" of the definition of F, with the actual dimensions substituted for the formal dimensions and the actual parameters substituted for the formal parameters. In the simple example given above, the Calling Rule allows us to replace the occurrence of `sum(2,3)` by the result of substituting `2` for `x` and `3` for `y` in `x+y`. In other words, it allows us to replace `sum(2,3)` by `2+3`, as desired.

The notion of a "relevant" call is defined in almost the same way as it was in the definition of free occurrences given earlier. The calls relevant to a definition are those appearing in the subject or in the right-hand side of a definition in the body, provided there is no "intervening" definition in some subclause. For example, in the expression

```
h(x) + f(y)
 where
  x = y*g + 5
       where
        g = p - f(q*a + y);
        q = k(3,z);
        k(a,b) = a*a + f(b*b);
       end;
  y = f(u) - u
       where
        f(d) = d*d - 5;
        u = 135;
       end;
  f(t) = (t-a)*(t+y);
 end
```

the "calls" `f(y)`, `f(q*a + y)`, and `f(b*b)` are all relevant to the definition

```
f(t) =(t-a)*(t+y);
```

but the call `f(u)` is not. The definition relevant to this last call is

```
f(d) = d*d - 5;
```

because (as before) the innermost definition has precedence.

The Calling Rule allows us to "expand" the first two calls, so that the resulting term will be

```
h(x) + (y-a)*(y+y)
 where
  x = y*g + 5
       where
        g = p - ((q*a+y) - a)*((q*a+y) + y);
        q = k(3,z);
        k(a,b) = a*a + f(b*b);
       end;
  y = f(u) - u
       where
        f(d) = d*d - 5;
        u = 135;
       end;
  f(t) = (t-a)*(t+y);
 end
```

Any attempt to expand the third call (f(b*b)), however, will result in a clash of variables. The definition

```
k(a,b) = a*a + f(b*b)
```

would become

```
k(a,b) = a*a + ((b*b)-a)*((b*b)+y);
```

and now the meaning has been changed. The variable a, which occurs as a "global" of the definition of f, has been introduced into a context in which it is also being used as a formal parameter. The proper, "outer", value is no longer available.

Individual examples of the "clash of variables" are usually easy to understand-once they have been pointed out. It is much harder for the unaided programmer to detect clashes in a moderately complicated program. Fortunately, it is not too difficult to formulate the precise regulations regarding permissible substitutions, and these rules can be easily implemented as a checking program. A programmer using the transformation rules would indicate to the program which call is to be expanded. The transformation program would check that no clashes would occur, and perform the expansion if it passed the check. Otherwise, it would tell the programmer exactly where the clash takes place. Programmers could therefore have absolute confidence in the correctness of their transformations, even if they themselves do not have a perfect grasp of the subtleties involved in the various restrictions on the transformation rules. (On the other hand, the people who implement the checking/transforming package must have a very good understanding of the rules. They would need a more detailed specification than that provided here.)

4.2.3 The Renaming Rules

The formal dimensions and formal parameters of a function definition are sometimes called "dummy" dimensions and variables. The reason for this is that the choice of which dimension name or variable to use is (almost) of no importance. These dimensions and variables are just "dummies" that stand in for the actual dimensions and actual parameters of a call. The use of a dimension name like x as a formal dimension or a variable like x as a formal parameter does not involve any reference to any dimension x or any value that x may have in the context of the definition. The following rule captures this idea by permitting us to change these dimensions and variables.

The Formal Parameter Renaming Rule:

Let

$$\{F_1, F_2, .., F_k\}.a_0, a_1, .., a_{m-1}(P_0, P_1, ..., P_{n-1}) = E;$$

be a definition appearing in the body of a where clause and let $c_0, c_1, ..c_{m-1}$ be a new sequence of distinct dimension names and $Q_0, Q_1, ..Q_{n-1}$ be a new sequence of distinct nulladic variables. Then the above definition can be replaced by

$$\{F_1, F_2, .., F_k\}.c_0, c_1, .., c_{m-1}(Q_0, Q_1, ..., Q_{n-1}) = E';$$

where E' is the result of (simultaneously) replacing each free occurrence in E of any a_i with the corresponding c_i and replacing each free occurrence in E of any P_i with the corresponding Q_i, provided no clashes of dimensions or variables result.

With this rule, clashes could arise if one of the Q's is substituted into a context in which it is bound.

This rule could, for example, be used on the term given earlier to transform the definition

```
k(a,b) = a*a + f(b*b);
```

into the definition

```
k(n,m) = n*n + f(m*m);
```

and this change would allow us to apply the Calling Rule to the call of `f`.

There are similar rules, the Local Variable Renaming Rule and the Local Dimension Renaming Rule, for changing the local variables and local dimensions (those which are defined or declared) in a where clause.

4.2.4 The Addition and Elimination Rules

It should be apparent that repeated use of the Calling rules may sometimes result in the complete elimination of relevant occurrences of the variable or dimension in question. In such a case the definition that was used becomes "redundant." The Elimination Rule allows us to eliminate such redundant definitions or declarations.

The Definition/Declaration Elimination Rule

Let *W* be a where clause and *D* a definition or declaration in the body of *W* that defines a variable `V` or declares a new dimension `V`. If `V` does not occur free in the subject of *W* or in any definition in the body of *W*, then *W* may be replaced by the clause *W'* formed by removing *D* from the body of *W*.

We have already seen that using the renaming rules allowed us to expand all three calls of `f` in the term given earlier, yielding

```
h(x) + (y-a)*(y+y)
 where
  x = y*g + 5
       where
        g = p - ((q*a+y) - a)*((q*a+y) + y);
        q = k(3,z);
        k(m,n) = m*m + ((n*n)-a)*((n*n)+z);
       end;
  y = f(u) - u
       where
        f(d) = d*d - 5;
        u = 135;
       end;
  f(t) = (t-a)*(t+z);
 end
```

The Elimination Rule allows us to eliminate the (now useless) definition

```
f(t) = (t-a)*(t+z);
```

and transform the above into

```
h(x) + (y-a)*(y+y)
 where
  x = y*g + 5
       where
        g = p - ((q*a+y) - a)*((q*a+y) + y);
        q = k(3,z);
        k(m,n) = m*m + ((n*n)-a)*((n*n)+z);
       end;
  y = f(u) - u
       where
        f(d) = d*d - 5;
        u = 135;
       end;
 end
```

It should be apparent that a function definition can be expanded out of a program in this way only if it is nonrecursive (i.e., only if the function is not defined in terms of itself either directly or indirectly). If a program has no recursive function definitions, then all function definitions can be removed eventually. Among other things, this means that an implementation of `Lucid` without functions can be converted into an implementation of a slightly extended language in which at least nonrecursive definitions are allowed. We just add a front end to the existing implementation. The new front end expands all the calls to the functions, then hands the resulting program over to the existing implementation.

The Elimination Rule, like all of the transformation rules, can be applied in reverse. The inverse rule (which we will call the Addition Rule) says that any definition or declaration can be added to the body of the clause provided there are (in the subject or the other definitions) no relevant occurrences of the variable being defined or dimension being declared, and provided the variable, function, or dimension is not already a local of the clause. Once the definition is added, we can use the Calling Rule in reverse and introduce some calls to the function. This process could be thought of as increasing the "modularity" of the program. Suppose, for example, that a clause contains the expressions `x**2+b*x+c`, `(x+1)**2+b*(x+1)+c`, and `(y-z)**2+b*(y-z)+c`. We could introduce the function definition

```
f(v) = v**2+b*v+c;
```

and replace the three expressions by `f(x)`, `f(x+1)`, and `f(y-z)`. The restrictions on the Calling Rule (which still must hold when the rule is used in reverse) ensure that `b` and `c` have the same meanings in the three expressions as they do in the new definition.

The determined use of the elimination rules can very often produce where clauses with empty bodies. As a simple example, the expression

```
sum(3,5)
 where
  sum(x,y) = x + y;
 end
```

can be transformed to

```
3 + 5
 where
  sum(x,y) = x + y;
 end
```

using the Calling rule, and then to

```
3 + 5
 where
 end
```

with the Elimination Rule. It seems only natural that we should be able to discard the useless `where` and `end`. This is in fact the case.

4.3 Program Verification

We will now reason about several of the programs contained in Chapter 1 and about one program we haven't so far seen.

Most of this reasoning will be based on properties of the `Lucid` operators and constants such as `first`, `next`, `@`, and `#`. These properties will be stated when needed, rather than start off with a necessarily incomplete and over-full list of them.

Surprisingly, perhaps, we will use induction sparingly. In `Lucid` programs, most uses of recursion are found in recursively defined variables; recursively defined functions are seldom seen (although the language definitely allows them). Several of the example programs we have seen do not use recursion at all, for example the matrix transposition and the matrix multiplication programs (except that the latter *does* use recursion in the definition of summation). In general, the use of induction in proofs of programs mirrors the use of recursion in the programs being proved.

4.3.1 Matrix Transposition

Consider the following definition of a variable `Z` that will hold the transpose of matrix `A`

```
Z = realign.t,x(realign.x,y(realign.y,t(A)))
  where
      dimension t;
      realign.a,b(C) = C @.a #.b;
  end
```

How do we reason about transposition when it is defined without using subscripts? Answer: we don't use subscripts in the program, but we do use subscripts in the proof. To verify that `Z` denotes the transpose of `A`, all we have to do is show that `(Z @.x i) @.y j = (A @.x j) @.y i`, for arbitrary `i` and `j`. To do this we add

the assumption that `i` and `j` are arbitrary to the annotation of the outermost level, and import the property (that they exist) into the annotation of the where clause. Inside the where clause we will prove that
`(realign.t,x(realign.x,y(realign.y,t(A))) @.x i) @.y j`
`= (A @.x j) @.y i`, which will imply that `(Z @.x i) @.y j`
`= (A @.x j) @.y i` inside the where clause, and we can export that to the outer level, since it doesn't refer to locals of the where clause (i.e., to `t` or `realign`). Of course, at the outer level, `i` and `j` are arbitrary.

So, here we go.

Inside the annotation of the where clause
`(realign.t,x(realign.x,y(realign.y,t(A))) @.x i) @.y j`
`= ((((A @.x #.t) @.y #.x) @.t #.y) @.x i) @.y j`
(using the Calling Rule for the definition of function `realign`)
`= ((((A @.x #.t) @.y #.x) @.x i) @.t #.y) @.y j`
(since x and t are different dimensions)
`= (((A @.x #.t) @.y i) @.t #.y) @.y j`
(since, for all `B`, `a`, `b`, and `k`, `(B @.a #.b) @.b k = B @.a k` provided `B` does not vary in dimension `b`, and, in this case, `A @.x #.t` does not vary in the `x` dimension)
`= (((A @.y i) @.x #.t) @.t #.y) @.y j`
(since `x` and `y` are different dimensions)
`= ((A @.y i) @.x #.y) @.y j`
(since `A @.y i` does not vary in dimension `t`)
`= (A @.y i) @.x j`
(since `A @.y i` does not vary in dimension `y`)
`= (A @.x j) @.y i`
(since `y` and `x` are different dimensions).

4.3.2 Matrix Multiplication

As mentioned in Chapter 1, matrix multiplication can be represented by a term

```
sum.z(A @.y #.z * B @.x #.z, n)
   where
      dimension z;
   end
```

Here, `sum.z(C, n)` is supposed to sum up the first `n` values of `C` in the `z` dimension. In fact, we will assume that `sum` works correctly, and show that the rest of the term is constructed appropriately. In particular, we will show that if

```
M = sum.z(A @.y #.z * B @.x #.z, n)
      where
         dimension z;
      end
```

then `(M @.x i) @.y k`
`= sum.z((A @.x i) @.y #.z) * (B @.x #.z) @.y k, n).`
This is expressing what we want because the first `n` values of `#.z` in the `z` dimension are `0` through `n-1`. (We are assuming that the matrices are loaded into `A` and `B` starting, in each dimension, at position `0`.) So, we are performing the summation for all `#.z` from `0` to `n-1`.

The proof proceeds as follows. We add to the annotation at the outermost level the assumption that `i` and `k` are arbitrary. We also add the trivially true property that
`(M @.x i) @.y k = (M @.x i) @.y k,`
and then import that into the annotation of the where clause. Now, in the where clause annotation, we use the Calling Rule with the definition of `M` and conclude the following:
`(M @.x i)@.y k`
`= (sum.z(A @.y #.z * B @.x #.z, n)@.x i @.y k`
`= sum.z(((A @.y #.z)@.x i)@.y k * ((B @.x #.z)@.x i)@.y k, n)`
(since `sum.z` works pointwise on all dimensions except `z`, in particular, on `x` and `y`)
`= sum.z(((A @.x i)@.y #.z)@.y k * ((B @.x #.z)@.x i)@.y k, n)`
(since dimensions `x` and `y` are different)
`= sum.z((A @.x i)@.y #.z * (B @.x #.z)@.y k, n)`
(since, for any `C`, `a`, `b` and `d`, `(C @.d a)@.d b = C @.d a`)
This, of course, is exactly what we were aiming for.

4.3.3 Tournament

There are many ways to write the function `add` for use in the matrix multiplication program. In Chapter 1, we used `runningSum` and we also gave a faster method, using a *tournament*. In this section we will show that the tournament method works. (We will not show here that it really is faster.)

The function add from Chapter 1 is given below. It uses a new dimension t to lay out the results, B, of each step of the tournament. The function is explained in Chapter 1. It really only works for n being a power of two, but there is a simple modification, that we will not consider here, that works for arbitrary n.

```
sum.u(A, n) =
   B @.t log n
      where
         dimension t;
         B = A fby.t
               firstOfPair.u(B) + secondOfPair.u(B);
         firstOfPair.v(C) = C @.v (#.v * 2);
         secondOfPair.v(C) =  C @.v (#.v * 2 + 1);
      end;
```

In order to prove that the program works we establish that, inside the where clause, the values of B at all the different points in dimensions t and u are the sum of different segments of the array A. In particular, we will show that the value of B at point j in dimension t and point k in dimension u is the sum of the values of A from point k*2**j to point (k+1)*2**j - 1. (Refer to Figure 1.2 in Chapter 1.) Thus, the value of the program at point 0 in dimension u (i.e., the value of B at point log n in dimension t and point 0 in dimension u) will be the sum of the values of A from point 0 through point n - 1 (in dimension u).

This property of B (call it **P**) can be expressed as follows:

```
B = A @.u
((#.u) * 2**(#.t) + ..  + A @.u ((#u + 1) * 2**(#.t) - 1)
```

It will be proved by *Lucid Induction* in dimension t. (We use induction in dimension t because B is defined recursively in dimension t.) All we have to do is prove that

1. first.t **P** is true, and that

2. **P** $\rightarrow$ next.t **P**.

To prove first.t **P**, we need to prove that

```
first.t B =
first.t(A @.u ((#.u) * 2**(#.t) +..+ A @.u
((#u+1)*2**(#.t)-1))
```

We shall do this by showing that both sides are equal to `A`. It is easy to show that `first.t B = A`; that comes directly from the definition of `A`.

```
first.t(A @.u ((#.u)*2**(#.t) +..+ A @.u ((#u+1)*2**(#.t)-1))
= A @.u
((#.u)*2**first.t(#.t) +..+ A @.u ((#u+1)*2**first.t(#.t)-1))
```
(since nothing in that term except `#.t` varies in dimension `t`)
```
  = A @.u ((#.u)*2**0 +..+ A @.u ((#u+1)*2**0 - 1))
```
(since, for all `a`, `first.a (#.a) = 0`)
```
= A @.u ((#.u) +..+ A @.u ((#u+1)-1))
```
(since `2**0 = 1`) `= A @.u #.u`
```
= A
```

To prove that **P** → `next.t` **P**, we add to the annotation the assumption **P** and then try to prove `next.t` **P**. (When we do so, we will then discharge the assumption, giving the required implication.)

We therefore assume that
```
B = A @.u ((#.u)*2**(#.t) +..+ A @.u ((#u+1)*2**(#.t)-1)
```
To prove that `next.t` **P**, we will show that
```
next.t B =
next.t(A @.u ((#.u)*2**(#.t) +..+ A @.u ((#u+1)*2**(#.t)-1))
```
by showing that each side equals the same thing.
Now, by the definition of `B`,
```
next.t B = firstOfPair.u(B) + secondOfPair.u(B)
= B @.u (#.u * 2) + B @.u (#.u * 2 + 1)
```
(using the Calling Rule for `firstOfPair` and `secondOfPair`)
```
= (A @.u((#.u)*2**(#.t) +..+ A
@.u((#u+1)*2**(#.t-1)))@.u(#.u*2) +
(A @.u((#.u)*2**(#.t) +..+ A
@.u((#u+1)*2**(#.t-1)))@.u(#.u*2+1)
```
(using our last assumption (the inductive assumption) and the Calling Rule)
```
= (A @.u ((#.u*2)*2**(#.t)) +..+ A @.u ((#u*2+1)*2**(#.t-1)))
+
(A @.u ((#.u*2+1)*2**(#.t)) +..+ A @.u ((#u*2+2)*2**(#.t-1)))
= (A @.u ((#.u*2)*2**(#.t)) +..+ A @.u ((#u*2+2)*2**(#.t-1)))
```
Now,
```
next.t(A @.u ((#.u)*2**(#.t) +..+ A @.u ((#u+1)*2**(#.t)-1))
= A @.u ((#.u)*2**(#.t+1) +..+ A @.u ((#u+1)*2**(#.t+1)-1))
```
Thus, we have shown that **P** is true.

Running Standard Deviation

We close this chapter by presenting (in outline) an example of how the verification and transformation rules can be used together to massage a nontrivial (though still simple) program into an equivalent but very different form that performs the calculations using a very different algorithm.

The programs we will be working with all compute a "running" (in dimension d) standard deviation of their input: the output at point j in d will be the standard deviation

$$\sqrt{(\sum_{i=0}^{j}(a_i - \sum_{i=0}^{j} a_i/(j+1))^2)/(j+1)}$$

of the sequence $a_0, a_1, ..., a_j$ of values input so far.

Our first version is intended to be obviously correct, if inefficient.

```
sqrt(realign.t,d(
     avg.t((aa - avg.d(a))*(aa - avg.d(a)))
                           where
                             dimension t;
                             aa = realign.d,t(a);
                           end)
  where
    avg.k(y)    = s/(#.k + 1)
                  where
                    s = y fby.k s + next.k y;
                  end;
  end
```

It uses a naive algorithm and imitates as closely as possible the specification of the problem given above. With every number input it gets the new average of the numbers seen so far (to do this it keeps a running sum of the numbers), and then it goes back to the beginning-*rewinds*-and runs through all the input it has seen so far to compute the average of the square of how the input has differed from the new average. The square root of that number is then the standard deviation at the current point. (For each input a in dimension d, all the input to that point is laid out as aa, in temporary dimension t using function realign.d,t. The calculation is then done in dimension t, and the result is put back in dimension d, using realign.t,d.) The algorithm is quadratic in both time and space. Our goal is to transform it into a *linear* algorithm that uses *constant* space. Our first step is to prove that avg is linear, that is, that it distributes through addition and subtraction. This is a lengthy but straightforward task; we will not present it here.

Then we use the binomial theorem to expand the square of aa - avg.d(a) and the subject of the subject becomes

```
realign.t,d(avg.t(
  aa*aa - 2*aa*avg.d(a) + avg.d(a)*avg.d(a)))
```

Since avg is linear, we can reduce this to

```
realign.t,d(
   avg.t(aa*aa) - avg.t(2*aa*avg.d(a)) +
   avg.t(avg.d(a)*avg.d(a)))
```

We can also prove, without much difficulty, that avg.t(avg.d(a)*avg.d(a)) is avg.d(a)*avg.d(a) and that avg.t(2*aa*avg.d(a)) is 2*avg.t(aa)*avg.d(a) (because neither avg.d(a) nor 2 vary in dimension t). The subject of the subject becomes

```
realign.t,d(
  avg.t(aa*aa) - 2*avg.t(aa)*avg.d(a) +
  avg.d(a)*avg.d(a))
```

and we can use the Calling Rule on aa to give

```
realign.t,d(
  avg.t(realign.d,t(a)*realign.d,t(a)) -
  2*avg.t(realign.d,t(a))*avg.d(a) +
  avg.d(a)*avg.d(a))
```

We can now distribute realign.t,d through its argument, giving

```
realign.t,d(avg.t(realign.d,t(a)*realign.d,t(a))) -
realign.t,d(2*avg.t(realign.d,t(a))*avg.d(a)) +
realign.t,d(avg.d(a)*avg.d(a))
```

Now, using the facts that realign.a,b is the identity when applied to something that doesn't vary in dimension a and that realign.a,b(f.a(realign.b,a(A))) is equal to f.b(A) when A doesn't vary in dimension a and a and b are not global dimensions of the definition of f, we get

```
avg.d(a*a) - 2*avg.d(a)*avg.d(a)) + avg.d(a)*avg.d(a)
```

The whole program is now (after some cleaning up of the subject of the subject)

```
sqrt(avg.d(a*a) - avg.d(a)*avg.d(a))
 where
  avg.k(y)  = s/(#.k + 1)
              where
               s = a fby.k s + next.k a;
              end;
 end
```

The program no longer rewinds its input to produce each output value, and does not need unbounded storage. Yet it could still be improved. We can use the Calling Rule, expand all the calls to **avg** and then discard the definition. Next we can use a rule to combine all the clauses into one, and introduce some new variables for convenience. The manipulations are completely straightforward and eventually produce

```
sqrt(s2/n - (s1/n)*(s1/n))
 where
  s2 = a*a fby.d s2 + next.d a*a;
  s1 = a fby.d s1 + next.d a;
  n = (#.d + 1);
 end;
```

This version is essentially the same as the previous one, but now it is clearer that it is using a more sensible algorithm. Instead of saving all its input and repeatedly rereading it, it keeps running sums of the input values and their squares. Its memory requirements are bounded, and the amount of work performed is now linear in the amount of input.

Of course, the transformation need not stop here. The program is still numerically naive, because it is subtracting larger and large quantities. If we introduce the new definition `D = s2*n - s1*s1;` we can clean up the subject:

```
sqrt(d)/n
 where
  D = s2*n - s1*s1;
  s2 = a*a fby.d s2 + next.d a*a;
  s1 = a fby.d s1 + next.d a;
  n = #.d + 1;
 end;
```

Now we change the program to compute `D` incrementally, rather than directly. Using the (easily derived) annotations

```
D = first.d D fby.d D + (next.d D - D)
first D = 0
next D - D = (n*a - 2*s1)*a + s2
```

we can modify the definition of `D` to be

```
D = 0 fby (n*a - 2*s1) + s2;
```

and even better improvements are possible.

The improvements in the performance of the new version are real in any implementation. The difference between the linear and quadratic algorithms is very noticeable. The interpreter always saves its input (because demands for input values are, in general, unpredictable). Thus, the new version running on its own will still require more and more buckets in the memory. However, if the program was converted to a filter (so that the values of `a` were not coming directly from the "outside world"), the difference would be noticeable. A filter based on the original algorithm would endlessly redemand early values of its input and prevent the interpreter's garbage collector from collecting the buckets. The new version would not "revisit" its input, and eventually these buckets would be retired and collected if they were not being used elsewhere.

The objection could be made that the programs are not really equivalent, because rounding errors will cause different values to be produced. This is certainly the case, and indeed the last transformation was made with the *intention* of getting different, better output. However, this does not mean that formal equivalence between programs computing with approximations to real numbers is an unrealistic concept. In general it will be true that transformed programs will give different results in spite of being formally equivalent. Nevertheless, if we have used the transformation rules correctly, we can be confident that any differences between the programs are due *solely to rounding errors.* If the original was correct "in theory" then so is the second, and any problems can be blamed on errors in calculation. This knowledge can be extremely useful. Otherwise, if a numerical program does not work, there is no simple way to decide whether a logical error is at fault (and debugging is required) or whether the numerical techniques are inadequate. The presence of numerical inaccuracy makes formal transformation and verification more, not less important. Program bugs are much harder to find through testing because the random numerical errors provide excellent camouflage.

4.4 Summary

One of the strengths of Lucid is that it can be *thought of* as a formal system for verifying and reasoning about programs—one in which proving correctness of somewhat complicated programs would be possible.

Using a simple example, we showed how Lucid verification techniques are similar to functional programming verification techniques in the referential transparency of assertions. We also showed how Lucid verification techniques are similar to procedural programming verification techniques in the forms of assertions and proofs.

We have described four types of rules for meaning-preserving transformation of Lucid programs on which a formal verification system could be built. These include the Basis rule, the Calling rule, the Renaming rules, and the Addition and Elimination rules.

The program transformation rules given in this chapter allow only a very limited kind of formal reasoning *about* programs. Yet they are very useful as part of a formal system for verifying programs, a system that allows annotations of programs to be derived and manipulated. We went back and revisited some of the programs given earlier (in Chapter 1), and proved that they are working as intended. We even introduced a new program that is obviously correct but inefficient (quadratic), and showed how it could be transformed, using derived properties, into an equivalent, efficient program with linear performance.

Chapter 5

Eduction

We know what a `Lucid` program means mathematically (see Chapter 3), yet that in itself does not suggest a particular model of computation for deriving the same meaning operationally. The purpose of this chapter is to consider the various ways that Lucid programs can be evaluated and to describe in detail the most appropriate model of computation, namely, *eduction.*

Previously, we have seen that `Lucid` programs can be viewed globally in geometrical terms or locally in elemental terms. Both these views are equally valid as mental devices to enable the programmer to conceive and understand `Lucid` programs. And each view suggests its own family of computing models—extensional models that embody the global geometrical view and intensional models that embody the local elemental view.

Before we compare these two approaches to evaluating `Lucid` programs, it is worth relating the operational semantics given by a model of computation to the mathematical semantics. Since `Lucid` is purely declarative, the correct meaning of a `Lucid` program is that which is given mathematically. This is done without appealing to any operational notions [8]. Thus, the mathematical semantics of a `Lucid` program has primacy over the many operational semantics that can be given to the `Lucid` program using different models of computations. Consequently, the correctness of a model of computation is determined by its ability to operationally give semantics to `Lucid` programs that coincide with their mathematical semantics.

5.1 Extensional and Intensional Models

Let us consider an extensional model of computation called *reduction* [37]. It is the standard model for evaluating declarative programs, and more specifically, functional programs. In reduction, programs are considered to be expressions, and a program is evaluated by repeatedly transforming, or reducing, the expression into a possibly simpler expression. The original expression must include any data that the program is to work on, so that at every stage we are manipulating both program and data, and the two become intimately entwined. The process stops when no further transformation can be applied. At each stage, several transformations may be possible, but it doesn't matter which we apply. If we get an answer, we always get the same answer, but it is possible to make choices so that we do not arrive at the answer. There usually are simple tests to apply, when making choices, to ensure that we are making choices that are leading in the right direction.

Graph reduction [37] is a form of reduction where the expressions at each stage are represented by graphs. This makes sense: for example, if a variable is used (not defined) at several places in a program (and thus at several places in the expression), in the graph representation all these uses can be linked, or point, to one place. Changing what is being pointed to has the effect of making several changes in the expression simultaneously. The graph representation is much more efficient. For our discussion, the important thing to realize is that graph reduction involves building and changing a generally large and complicated data structure.

If graph reduction were used to evaluate `Lucid` programs, the nonpointwise operators would be treated as sequence-manipulating operators, such as `cons` for `fby` and `tail` for `next`. In the lazy graph reduction computing model, the following `Lucid` definition

```
x = 1 fby.time next.time x fby.time x + 1;
```

would be considered as

```
x = cons(1, cons(head tail x, x+1))}
```

with `+` being a lazy coercion, to the sequence domain, of the addition operator on the basic domain. The operator `cons` is completely lazy, and evaluates neither argument until its value is needed. For example, if a program containing the `Lucid` definition of `x` is to give a defined result, the even elements of `x` must never be needed. However, if the odd elements *are* needed, a linear list structure or graph is built up in which every other element (the second, fourth, sixth, etc.) is a subgraph that corresponds to the first argument of the second call of `cons` in the program (i.e., `head tail x`). These subgraphs are like suspended computations; they are never developed. It is important to realize that a large connected data structure is built up for `x`, with much of it consisting of suspended computations.

Now let us contrast reduction (which typifies an extensional model of computation) with an intensional model of computation that embodies a local elemental view of computation [46]. At the core of an intensional computing model is a fundamentally distributed view of both computation and data. An intensional computing model makes sense of `Lucid` programs that do not, at each context, make everything explicit. The model knows, at each context, the appropriate implicit context. In fact, in the intensional model, all that is known are the values of things in implicit contexts. When evaluating programs containing the equation `x = 1 fby.time next.time x fby.time x + 1`, for example, the model will know the values of `x` in particular contexts but it will not know what the whole of `x` is.

This means that the intensional computing model has no such thing as a connected data structure. For a program, containing the definition of `x` as stated above, that has a defined result, the needed values of `x` will be calculated but they will be connected together only abstractly, not concretely.

Each value that is calculated will be stored somewhere with a context indicating to which element of the sequence `x` it corresponds. Nothing will be stored for the even elements of `x`, because they are not needed and thus no attempts will have been made to calculate them. The needed values of `x` can be stored anywhere, even on different machines if the implementation is distributed, as it might well be. There is no monolithic or contiguous structure.

A novel aspect of the intensional computing model is that it allows random access into sequences. If a particular value of the (conceptual) sequence `x` is required, the context that is calculated is used to retrieve the value with that context. There is no traveling down a list to reach the point we want. The context itself will even indicate on where (which machine) to look if the implementation is distributed. (At an earlier stage, the context determines, in exactly the same way, where to store the value.) No coercion is involved with operators such as "+" which, semantically, are pointwise extensions of basic operators. What we are storing are context-augmented elements of the basic domain and we just apply conventional addition to elements with the same context (and return the result, with that context). It is characteristic of an intensional computing model that it is concerned with the elements and not the "big picture."

What an intensional computing model evaluates are values of a Lucid program at one or more contexts. Computing the value of the program (or result) at a context would require values of certain variables at appropriate contexts to be computed which, in turn, would require values of other variables at other appropriate contexts to be computed, and so on.

Consider the following program (which solves Laplace's equation in two dimensions (x,y) using a four-stencil relaxation method).

```
s where
    s = if ELECTRODE then POTENTIAL
                          else 0 fby.time avg(s) fi;
    avg(s) = ( (prev.x s + next.x s) +
               (prev.y s + next.y s) ) / 4;
  end
```

The value of the program is denoted by s, which is a two-dimensional sequence defined over dimension time. When the value s at context [time=T, [x=X,y=Y]] [1] (assuming Y,X,Y>0) is to be computed, it causes avg(s) to be computed at context [time=T-1, [x=X,y=Y]]. This, in turn, is the average of the values of s at context [time=T-1, [x=X-1,y=Y]], context [time=T-1, [x=X+1,y=Y]], context [time=T-1, [x=X,y=Y-1]], and context [time=T-1, [x=X,y=Y+1]]. To compute these values could require other values of s to be computed and the computation thus goes on.

An intensional computing model attempts to define the universe of values that the program denotes by simultaneously or incrementally generating these values at various contexts. Thus, as values of the above program at different contexts need to be computed, values of s at other contexts that are required to compute the needed values are computed. For example, if the value of the program at context [time=10, [x=25,y=50]] is needed, values of s at contexts T,X,Y are needed where $0 \le T < 10$, $25-(10-T) \le X \le 25+(10-T)$, and $50-(10-T) \le Y \le 50+(10-T)$.

An intensional computing model views the defining of the universe of values corresponding to the program to be fundamentally a

[1]For context specification, we adopt the convention that the name of the dimension denotes the point in that dimension (e.g., time denotes #.time).

distributed activity. That is, instead of treating the universe of values as a monolithic structure, it treats values as being independent of one another but with a relationship being given by the relationship between the respective contexts. Specifically, computing the value of `s` at context `[time=T, [x=X,y=Y]]` can be conducted independent of computing the value of `s` at context `[time=T+1, [x=X+1,y=Y+1]]` although, in this case, the latter would require the former to be computed.

5.2 Intensional Computing Models

There are many possible intensional models of computation to evaluate `Lucid` programs. There is a simple way in which these models can be distinguished: by how each model goes about computing the desired results of a program [24]. Specifically, they can be distinguished

- when each value (of a variable/term at a context) of a program is *selected* to be computed; and
- when these selections are made relative to each other.

A value being selected to be computed simply means that the value can, from then on, be computed from values it depends on when they in turn are available. Conversely, a value that has not been selected to be computed cannot be defined even if it can be computed.

This simple distinction can be used to uniquely characterize different intensional computing models. Consider an intensional model (which we call *random*) in which values to be computed are selected randomly:

> Repeatedly select a value to be computed by selecting a random variable or term of the program and a random context meaningful to the program.

For example, if it was desired that the value of the Laplacian relaxation program at context `[time=10, [x=25,y=50]]` be computed, the random computing model would eventually select that value to be computed. That in itself would not necessarily mean that the value will actually be computed soon after. It would only be computed after all the values that it depends on have been (randomly) selected and computed. This may take unbounded yet finite time.

The universe of values denoted by the program is increasingly defined since progress is made in repeatedly selecting to compute a random variable at a random context. However, producing the desired result would take an unbounded yet finite number of selections.

Here is another intensional model which we refer to as the *eager* computing model:

> Instantly select all values of the program to be computed.

Although we do not prove it here, with the eager model, the results of the program are computed as soon as possible. Additionally, an unbounded number of superfluous values[2] could also be computed.

If it was desired that the value of the Laplacian relaxation program at context `[time=10, [x=25,y=50]]` be computed, it would occur as soon as possible. This is because all values of `s` are selected to be computed at the initial stage and each value of `s` is computed as soon as the values it depends on are computed. Therefore, the value of `s` at context `[time=10, [x=25,y=50]]` is computed as soon as the values of `s` at context `[time=9, [x=24,y=50]]`, context `[time=9, [x=26,y=50]]`, context `[time=9, [x=25,y=51]]`, and context `[time=9, [x=25,y=49]]` are computed. However, even if that is the only value needed by the outside world, all values that can be computed will be computed resulting in unbounded amount of superfluous computation. In practice, one almost always restricts the extent to which superfluous values are computed by suitable throttling mechanisms.

Here is yet another intensional model which we refer to as the *piped* computing model.

- Initially, select values associated with all variables of the program at the initial context to be computed.

- Subsequently, select a value of a variable at a context to be computed when the variable at the preceding context has been defined.

Unlike the random and eager computing models, the piped computing model requires that the value of a variable at a given context has to be defined before any of the values of the variable at succeeding contexts can be computed. Thus, to compute the value of the Laplacian relaxation program at context `[time=10, [x=25,y=50]]`, all

[2]A value is considered *superfluous* if it does not determine a desired output.

values at "earlier" contexts would have to be selected and computed first even though many of them are unrelated and unnecessary and, in some cases, undefinable.

Consider the following definition

```
x = 1 fby.time next.time x fby.time 1;
```

With the piped model, if the value of `x` at context `[time=2]` were needed, it would first require the value of `x` at `[time=0]` to be produced before the value of `x` at `[time=1]` is selected to be computed. However, for this value to be computed requires the value of `x` at `[time=2]`; this is not possible with the piped model since for the value of `x` at `[time=2]` to be selected, the value of `x` at `[time=1]` has to be computed.

Each of the intensional models we discussed so far have certain drawbacks that make them impractical. The random model is clearly only of theoretical interest. The eager model results in superfluous computation and the piped model does not always compute correctly. The model that we will discuss next is correct and it does not result in any superfluous computation.

5.3 The Eduction Computing Model

The word *eduction* is defined in the Oxford English Dictionary as follows. "The action of drawing forth, eliciting, or developing from a state of latent, rudimentary, or potential existence; the action of educing (principles, results of calculations) from the data."

Eduction [3] can be described as follows.

- Select only those values of the result that are known to be needed by the outside world.
- Select values of variables that are used in computing values of previously selected values of variables.

Consider when the value of the Laplacian relaxation program is needed at `[time=10, [x=25,y=50]]` by the outside world. The value of `s` at context `[time=10, [x=25,y=50]]` is computed. This causes `avg(s)` to be computed at context `[time=9, [x=25,y=50]]`. This, in turn, is the average of the values of `s` at contexts `[time=9, [x=26,y=50]]`, `[time=9, [x=24,y=50]]`, `[time=9, [x=25,y=49]]`, and `[time=9, [x=25,y=51]]`. To compute these values could require other values of `s` to be computed and can be done similarly.

In computing other values, it is possible that some of the values are already available as they have been computed in computing another result. For example, computing values of `s` at contexts `[time=t, [x=i-1,y=j]]`, and `[time=t, [x=i+1,y=j]]` both require the value of `s` at context `[time=t-1, [x=i,y=j]]`. Instead of computing this value afresh each time, it could be computed only if it has not been computed before, and retained for future use until it is no longer needed in computing other values.

We can replace the abstract notion of "value selection" that we used in describing the various intensional models with the concrete notion of "value demand." Thus, demand for a value is an explicit request for that value to be computed as soon as possible. And a demand is satisfied when the value being demanded has been computed.

We can now restate the eduction model as follows.

1. Need for a result value by the outside world causes it to be demanded.

2. If a value `e` at context `[c]` is demanded at some stage, then and only then are values demanded that are known to directly determine value `e` at context `[c]`.

Consider the following definition:

```
x = ( if p then a else b fi ) * y
```

Demand for value of $x_{[i]}$ (value of `x` at context `[i)` causes demands for values of $p_{[i]}$ and $y_{[i]}$ because only these values are known to determine value $x_{[i]}$. Assuming that value $p_{[i]}$ is defined and it is `TRUE`, the value $a_{[i]}$ can be demanded subsequently since this value is now known to determine value of $x_{[i]}$. Then, the value of $x_{[i]}$ is the value of $a_{[i]}$.

The eduction model only does useful computation since it does not compute values that are not needed to compute a result. In the above example, observe that eduction avoids the computation of value $b_{[i]}$, which is useless when $p_{[i]}$ is `TRUE`.

Eductive Evaluation

To give the reader a better understanding of eduction, let us consider how the eduction model would evaluate a more elaborate program, namely, the matrix multiplication program (which we saw in Chapters 1 and 3). The program computes the product of two matrices, `A` and `B` (defined over `x` and `y` dimensions), which is denoted by `C`.

```
C where
  C = sum.z(product,n)
    where
      dimension z;
      product = realign.y,z(A) * realign.x,z(B);
      realign.u,v(C) = C @.u #.v;
      sum.u(X, n) = Y @.t log n
        where
          dimension t;
          Y = X fby.t
              firstOfPair.u(Y) +
              secondOfPair.u(Y);
          firstOfPair.v(Z) = Z @.v (#.v * 2);
          secondOfPair.v(Z) =  Z @.v (#.v * 2 + 1);
       end;
    end;
  end
```

It is useful to think of the program intensionally. That is, given the `x` and `y` dimension contexts, `C` using a binary summation (`sum`) of the inner product of the appropriate "row" of `A` (as denoted by the `x` context) and "column" of `B` (as denoted by the `y` context). The inner product itself (`realign.y,z(A) * realign.x,z(B)`) is defined for each `z`-context where `z` is a local dimension, orthogonal to dimensions `x` and `y`, to represent the inner-product vector.

Let us now see how eduction can be used to evaluate this program say for computing `C` at `x`-context `i` and `y`-context `j` assuming the value of `n` is `4`. This is simply the value of `sum.z(product,4)` at context `[z=0, [x=i,y=j]]` where `z` is a dimension local to the where clause enclosing the definition of `C`. Note that the value of the dimensional where clause expression is that of the subject expression when its local context (`z`) is set to 0.

Figure 5.1 illustrates the resulting propagation of demands and the eventual computation of values.

Demand for `sum.z(product,4)` at context `[z=0, [x=i,y=j]]` results in demand for `Y` at context `[t=2, [u=0, [x=i,y=j]]]`. (See Figure 5.2, part *(i)*.) Note that `u` is the formal dimensional parameter for `z` and that `t` is the dimension local to function `sum`.

Demand for `Y` at context `[t=2, [u=0, [x=i,y=j]]]` results in demands for `Y` at contexts `[t=1, [u=0, [x=i,y=j]]]` and `[t=1, [u=1, [x=i,y=j]]]`. (See

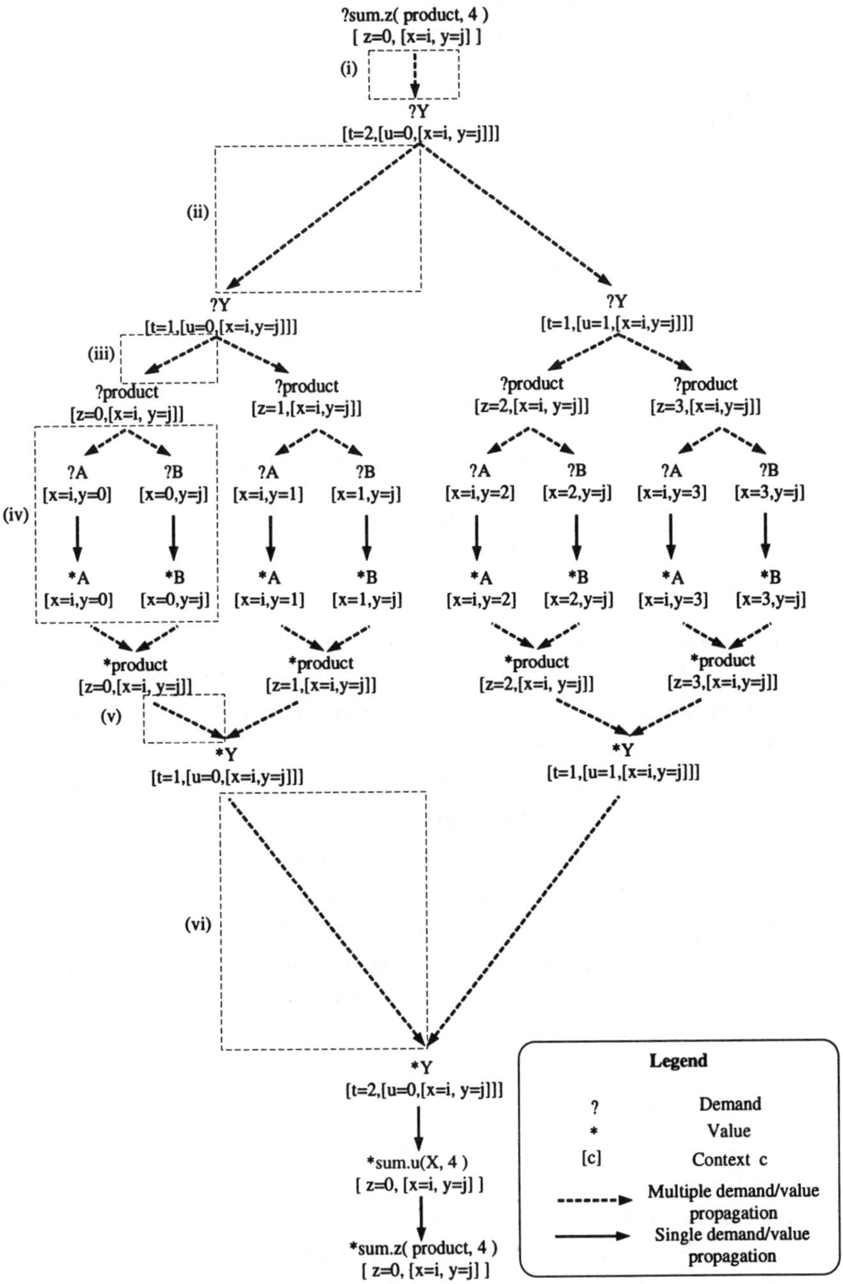

Figure 5.1: Eductive evaluation of matrix multiplication program

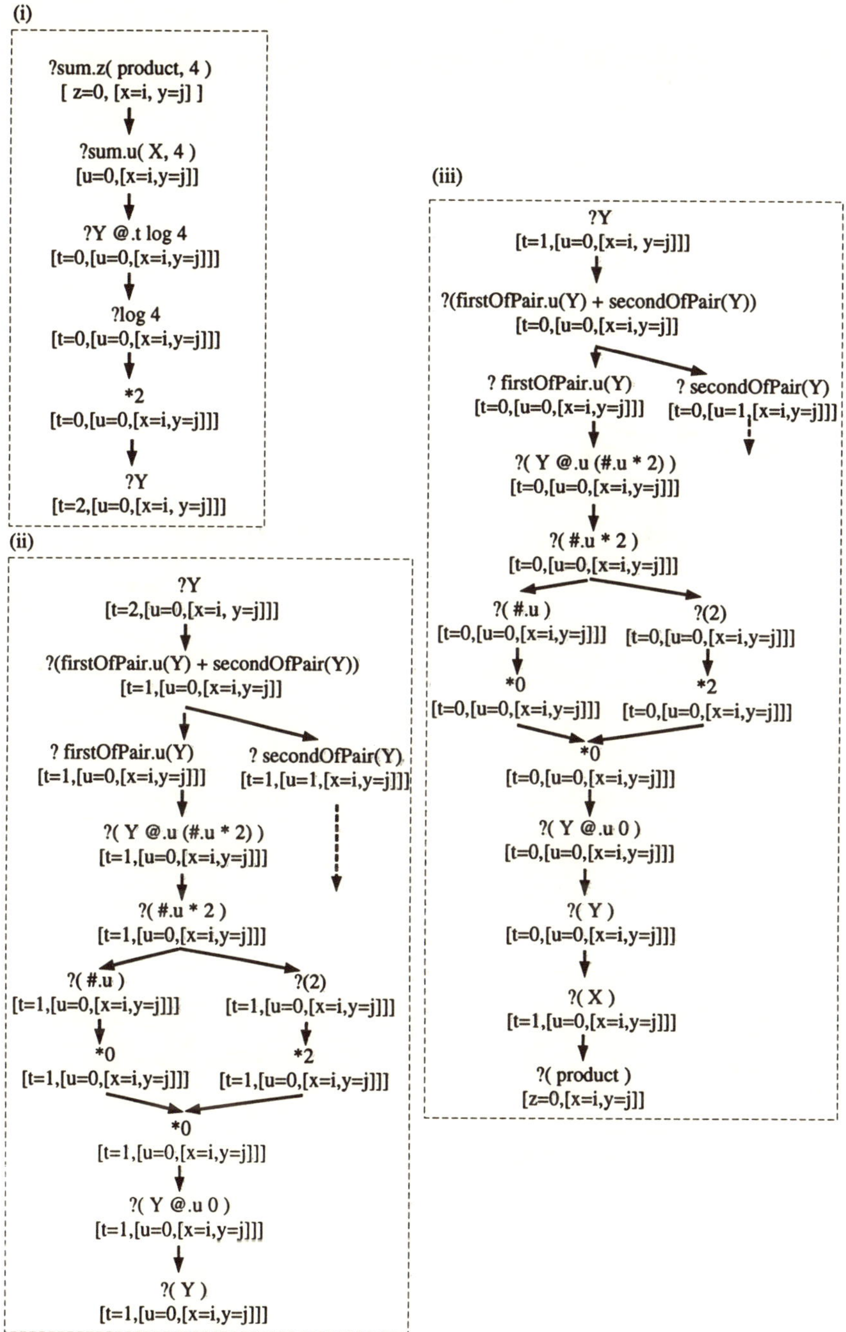

Figure 5.2: Detailed demand and value propagation (parts (i)–(iii))

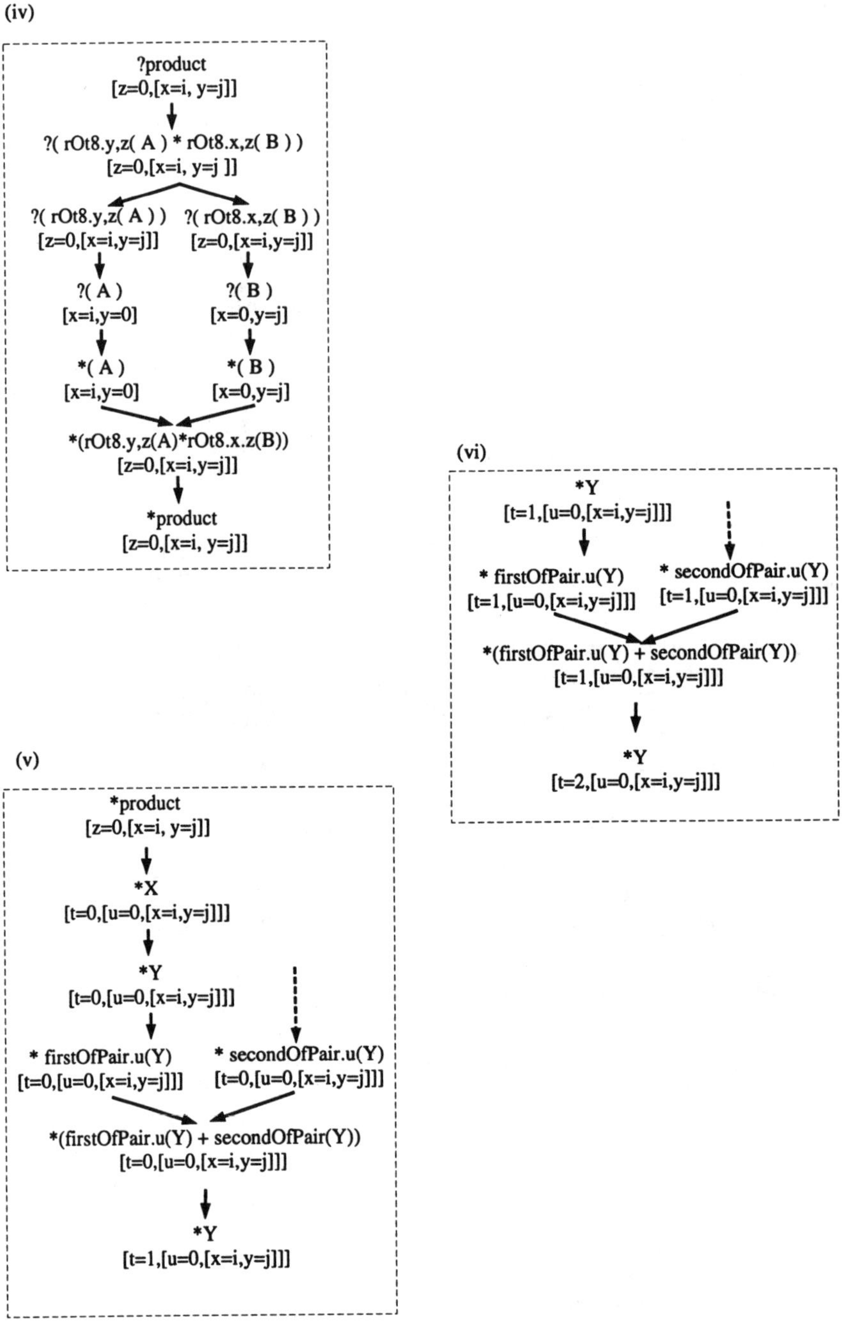

Figure 5.3: Detailed demand and value propagation (parts (iv)–(vi))

Figure 5.2, part *(ii)*.)

This, in turn, results in four demands for `product` at contexts `[z=0, [x=i,y=j]]`, `[z=1, [x=i,y=j]]`, `[z=2, [x=i,y=j]]`, and `[z=3, [x=i,y=j]]`. (See Figure 5.2, part *(iii)*.) Note that the context space for `product` does not include dimension `t` because of where `product` is defined. Also, note that the `z` context identifies the four values of the inner product vector.

Each demand for `product` results in demands for `A` and `B` at the appropriate `x` and `y` contexts. For example, demand for `product` at context `[z=3, [x=i,y=j]]` results in demands for `A` at context `[x=i,y=3]` and `B` at context `[x=3,y=j]`. (See Figure 5.3, part *(iv)*.) Assuming the appropriate values of `A` and `B` are immediately available, the four demanded products can be computed that would satisfy the four demands for `product`.

Once the four values of `product` at the different contexts are available, demands for `X` and `Y` at the associated contexts (`[t=0, [u=0, [x=i,y=j]]]`, `[t=0, [u=1, [x=i,y=j]]]`, `[t=0, [u=2, [x=i,y=j]]]`, and `[t=0, [u=3, [x=i,y=j]]]`) are satisfied. This, in turn, results in demands for `Y` at contexts `[t=1, [u=0, [x=i,y=j]]]`, and `[t=1, [u=1, [x=i,y=j]]]`) to be satisfied. (See Figure 5.3, part *(v)*.)

When two demands for `Y` when `t=1` are satisfied, the value of `Y` at context `[t=2, [u=0, [x=i,y=j]]]` can be satisfied. (See Figure 5.3, part *(vi)*.)

Finally, the value of `sum.z( product, 4)` at context `[z=0, [x=1,y=j]]` can be computed, which is the value of `C` at context `[x=i,y=j]` that was demanded originally.

Demand-driven versus Data-driven Execution

What we have described above is a purely demand-driven realization of eduction. This is generally necessary to deal with the "call-by-need" semantics needed to evaluate nonstrict and nonpointwise `Lucid` operators and functions.

Consider the evaluation of the following function, `stagger`

```
stagger.x( a, b ) =
   if a < b then (next.x a + b)
            else (a + next.x b) fi;
```

In evaluating `stagger.time(a,b)` at `time=t` it is not possible to predict without semantic examination of the function body whether values `a` at `time=t+1` and `b` at `time=t` or values `a` at `time=t` and `b` at `time=t+1` are needed to produce the needed value of `stagger`. Thus, a call-by-need semantics is necessary, which demand-driven execution implements.

The only reason to consider data-driven execution in place of demand-driven execution is to alleviate the expense of demand propagation when it is unnecessary and, consequently, inefficient.

Data-driven execution is not as general a mechanism as demand-driven execution. The difference loosely corresponds to the one between call-by-value semantics and call-by-need semantics.

For example, consider data-driven implementation of `if p then a else b fi`. Clearly, for the `if then else` operator to execute in a data-driven manner, all three of its arguments must be available (even though one is superfluous). For these arguments to be available, all three must have been selected for computation by the underlying computing model, which is not the case with eduction.

An even more difficult operator is the simple (nonpointwise) `@` operator as in `x @ y`. It is impossible to envision a data-driven implementation of this because the very value of `x` that is needed is determined by the value of `y`. In contrast, the `@` operator is naturally demand-driven: demand the value of `y` at the enclosing context and use that as the time-context to demand the value of `x`.

The only place where data-driven execution can be used is to evaluate "predictable" operators-the strict and pointwise operators such as `+`, `<` and nonpointwise operators such as `fby` and `next`. The reason is quite simple: for them it is possible to predict, without semantic examination of the operator, which argument values of the operator are necessary to produce a desired result.

Thus, data-driven execution can be used locally when possible and, when useful, with demand-driven execution being used everywhere else by default [24].

5.4 An Abstract Eduction Engine

We now describe how eductive evaluation can be applied mechanically by considering the design and operation of an abstract eduction engine [4, 6] (Figure 5.4).

The eductive evaluator that we describe consists of three components:

1. suspended operation component,

2. variable value component, and

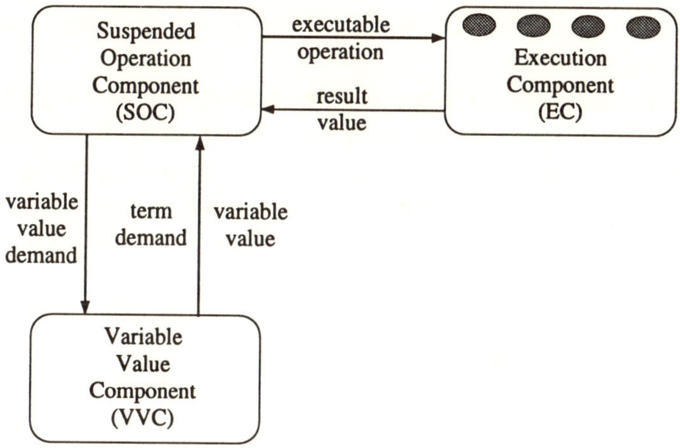

Figure 5.4: An abstract eduction engine architecture

3. execution component,

The suspended operation component (SOC) is responsible for demand propagation; the variable value component (VVC) is responsible for retaining values of variables that have been already computed; and the execution component (EC) is responsible for applying operations to their arguments to produce a result.

Program execution begins by a demand for a result value being made to the SOC. If the result is a term, the demand is processed at the SOC as described later. If the result is a variable, the VVC is checked to see if the demanded value has already been computed in which case it is returned satisfying the demand. If the value has not been computed, the term that defines the variable is demanded at the SOC.

When a term is demanded at the SOC, it causes the creation of a suspended operation, which is essentially the operation together with a set of place-holders for each argument of the operation. Each argument (which corresponds to a term or a variable) is demanded at the appropriate context as determined by the operation itself. For pointwise operators, the context of the operand values is the same as the context of the result being demanded. For nonpointwise operators, the context of the operand values are modified suitably to reflect the semantics of the operator. Thus, processing a demand at the SOC results in a suspended operation to be created and further demands to be propagated to the SOC when a term value is being demanded and to the VVC when a variable value is being demanded.

(A demand is immediately satisfied if the argument being demanded is a constant.)

When a demand for a value is processed at the VVC, it is determined if the value has already been computed. If so, the value is returned to the demander, which is a suspended operation in the SOC. If not, the name of the value is recorded in the VVC with its status set to "being computed" and the demand for its defining term is sent to the SOC, which is processed as described above. Further demands for the same value prior to its computation would cause them to be queued until the value is computed.

Values are returned to the SOC either by finding them in the VVC or when the arguments being demanded are constants (or inputs). When a value is demanded, the return address (the address of the specific suspended operation) is retained with the demand so that when the value is returned, it is inserted in the appropriate place.

When the required values are available at a suspended operation, it is unsuspended and sent for execution to the EC. The result produced by the EC is sent to the return address pointed to by the suspended operation, which could be another suspended operation in the SOC or it could be the value of a variable in the VVC. In the latter case, all pending demands for that variable value at the VVC are satisfied and returned to their respective return addresses.

The description of the eductive evaluator has been simplified in two respects: Firstly, when the operator being suspended is non-strict such as **if-then-else**, demand propagation is actually more complicated since it has to reflect the "sequential" nature of the operator. Secondly, we have not described how user-defined functions are evaluated mainly because it does not significantly add to the understanding of eductive evaluation.

An important aspect of the eductive evaluator is the management of values stored in the VVC. More precisely, deciding when variable values stored in the VVC can be discarded.

Consider the following expression

```
x where
    x = N fby.time x+y;
end
```

Each value of `x` is used twice and each value of `y` is used once whereas only the first value of `N` (i.e., `N` at context `time=0`) is used once; the rest are never used. We refer to the number of times a variable value is used as its *usage count.* When a variable value is stored in the VVC, its usage count is stored with it. Whenever a value is used (more precisely, retrieved from the VVC), its usage count is decremented by 1. When the usage count drops to 0, the value can be discarded as it is no longer needed.

Consider the example of matrix transposition first introduced in Chapter 1, which we present in a revised form.

```
Atrans where
    dimension t;
    Atrans = realign.t,x ( C );
    C = realign.x,y ( B );
    B = realign.y,t ( A );
  end
```

At first glance, it would appear that Lucid-style matrix transposition would require three times the storage required by conventional imperative matrix transposition. However, we note that each value of A, B, and C has usage count of 1. The effect is that when a value of Atrans has been evaluated at context x=X,y=Y,t=0, it would have used the value of C at context x=X,y=Y,t=X causing it to be discarded since its usage count is 0. Similarly, value of C at context x=X,y=Y,t=X would use value of B at context x=Y,y=Y,t=X causing it to be discarded and that would require the value of A at context x=Y,y=X,t=X, which would then be discarded. So, if demands for all values of Atrans are made simultaneously, at most twice the storage would be required at any time. This is precisely the same as would be required by a parallel in-place matrix transposition scheme.

So far we have assumed that the usage count of each variable value can be determined at compile time. However, generally this is not the case. Consider the following program

```
z where
    z = if p then x else y fi;
end
```

While the usage counts of values of z and p are 1, the usage count of values of x and y at a specific context cannot be determined without knowing the value of p at the same context. One approach is to assume that the usage counts of each value of x and y are 1. Whenever the value of p at a specific context is true, the usage count of x is correctly decremented when it is demanded. However, to discard the corresponding value of y (which will not be demanded), requires a "phantom" demand to be issued. The only purpose of a phantom demand is to decrement usage counts. While we do not explain this here, it is possible to construct programs where even the phantom demand propagation requires possibly unbounded superfluous computation just to correctly decrement usage counts.

The strategy that is used with most practical implementations of the eductive evaluator is some form of "retirement" scheme possibly in combination with the usage count scheme. The idea is as follows: Each value in the VVC is "aged" by the amount of time it has resided in the VVC since it was first created. When storage in the VVC is at a premium, the oldest values are discarded. This does not guarantee that any of the discarded values will not be needed again; if a discarded value is needed, it can be computed again assuming the input values to the program are available. The retirement strategy, which is a heuristic, can be combined with a deterministic yet incomplete scheme of precisely determining how many times a value of a variable will be needed. For those values with a precise usage count, they are discarded when the count reaches 0. For all other values, a retirement scheme is used to discard values.

5.5 Summary

`Lucid` programs can be given meaning operationally by using one of several models of computation. These models can be broadly categorized as extensional or intensional. Extensional models such as reduction, that view program evaluation globally in geometric terms, are not well suited to evaluating Lucid programs. Intensional models which view program evaluation locally in elemental terms are more compatible with `Lucid` programs. The most appropriate intensional model, called eduction, only performs useful computations in evaluating Lucid programs. We show how it is naturally realized using demand-driven execution and give an abstract architecture based on eduction.

Chapter 6

Parallelism and Fault Tolerance

The intensional nature of Lucid and eduction has two important practical consequences: (i) Lucid programs possess massive amounts of implicit parallelism and (ii) their evaluation can automatically tolerate faults. This chapter is devoted to explaining these two consequences. We start with massive implicit parallelism in Lucid programs.

6.1 Parallelism

6.1.1 Basic Forms of Parallelism

There are three forms of parallelism that arise in problem solving [13, 6]. The simplest form of parallelism, *functional parallelism*, is in the simultaneous execution of independent functions (or operators). This is sometimes referred to as structural parallelism or static parallelism. Consider the following Lucid program

```
x + y where
  x = 1 fby.time f(x);
  y = 0 fby.time g(y);
end
```

At each time-context, both x and y can be computed simultaneously since functions f and g can be independently invoked on their respective arguments.

The second form of parallelism, *temporal parallelism*, is due to pipelined processing of a temporal data sequence using a network of functions or operators. This is also referred to as stream parallelism or pipelined parallelism. Consider the following `Lucid` program

```
z where
  x = 1 fby.time f(x);
  y = g(x);
  z = h(y);
end;
```

(For simplicity, we assume that functions `f`, `g`, and `h` take the same amount of time to execute.) The values of `x` at successive `time`-contexts can only be computed serially since each value of `x` depends on its predecessor. However, when the value of `x` at context `time=i+1` is being computed using value of `x` at context `time=i`, the value of `y` at context `time=i` can be computed from the value of `x` at context `time=i` and the value of `z` at context `time=i-1` can be computed from the value of `y` at context `time=i-1`.

The third form of parallelism, *spatial parallelism*, is due to the simultaneous processing of elements of multidimensional data structures using the same function or operator. This is commonly referred to as data parallelism and is the source of massive parallelism. Consider the following `Lucid` program

```
z where
    dimension i,j;
    z = x + y;
  end;
```

It should be evident that each value of `z` at context `i,j` can be computed from the corresponding `x` and `y` values independent of other values of `z`. In effect, `x` and `y`, which denote two 2-dimensional data structures, can be added in a single step to produce the result matrix `z`.

It is possible to combine these different forms of parallelism. One such combination is *tournament parallelism* [5] —a hybrid of spatial and temporal parallelism as we shall see later.

6.1.2 Origin of Parallelism

`Lucid`, when it was first conceived in 1975, was principally designed to be a language to formally reason about programs [7]. Only in 1978 was it discovered that `Lucid` is, in fact, a dataflow language and, therefore, a language whose programs are implicitly parallel. The parallelism in `Lucid` (circa 1978) programs was both functional and temporal-values of independent variables at a given context could be simultaneously computed and values of dependent variables could be computed simultaneously over a moving window of contexts [45, 3].

It was not until 1985 that Lucid was extended to express spatial parallelism in addition to functional and temporal parallelism by allowing variables to vary in both time and multiple space dimensions [2]. It allowed a whole set of parallel algorithms to be directly expressed in Lucid-algorithms such as parallel bubble sort and parallel successive relaxation.

Since 1985, Lucid has continued to evolve and, in its present form, it can succinctly express diverse forms of parallelism including the three identified above: functional parallelism, temporal parallelism, and spatial parallelism.

The evolution of eduction as a model of parallel computation has mirrored that of Lucid. The first working interpreter of Lucid (originally developed in 1980 by C. Ostrum) embodied a sequential variant of the eduction model without exercising its latent ability to exploit parallelism. It was only starting in 1982 that the parallel capability of eduction was better understood. At this stage, eduction was seen as a model for exploiting both functional and temporal parallelism in Lucid programs that reflected the forms of parallelism that could then be expressed in Lucid. When Lucid was extended to express spatial parallelism, the corresponding extension to eduction to be able to exploit the parallelism was, in fact, natural. All it required was for contexts to be denoted by tuples of contexts rather than simply a temporal context.

6.1.3 Exploiting Parallelism in Lucid Programs

We use two examples, Laplacian relaxation and sorting, to illustrate how eduction exploits parallelism inherent in the respective Lucid programs.

Laplacian Relaxation Example

Consider the Laplacian relaxation example again.

```
s where
    s = if ELECTRODE then POTENTIAL
                    else 0 fby.time avg(s) fi;
    avg(s) = ( (prev.x s + next.x s) +
               (prev.y s + next.y s) ) / 4;
```

```
end
```

The program implicitly expresses all three forms of parallelism, the most apparent being spatial parallelism. Essentially, each value of `s` at a given time but at different `x` and `y` contexts can be computed simultaneously. That is, `s` at context `[time=t,[x=i,y=j]]` requires values of `s` at context `[time=t-1,[x=i',y=j']]` where `i',j'` denote neighboring points of point `(i,j)`. Each of these values can be demanded simultaneously causing their computation to proceed in parallel. Assuming `N` by `N` points of `s` are needed, the degree of spatial parallelism at each time step is $O(N^2)$ assuming all of the values from the previous time step are available and are accessible in constant time.

There is functional parallelism in the evaluation of `avg(s)` since two additions `prev.x s + next.x s` and `prev.y s + next.y s` can be performed simultaneously. This has the effect of doubling the degree of spatial parallelism.

There is also temporal parallelism implicitly expressed in the program. It is possible to generate the value of `s` at context `[time=t+1, [x=k,y=l]]` assuming its neighboring points from `time=t` are available. It is not necessary for all points of `s` to be defined at `time=t` only the neighboring points. Thus, certain portions of the two-dimensional object denoted by `s` can be more defined than others as a result of temporal parallelism.

Eduction exploits each of these parallelism as we show below. Demand for the value `s` at context `[time=T, [x=X,y=Y]]` causes `avg(s)` to be computed at context `[time=T-1, [x=X,y=Y]]`. This, in turn, depends on the values of `s` at contexts `[time=T-1, [x=X-1,y=Y]]`, `[time=T-1, [x=X+1,y=Y]]`, `[time=T-1, [x=X,y=Y-1]]`, and `[time=T-1, [x=X,y=Y+1]]`. These are demanded as a result of demanding `prev.x s + next.x s` at context `[time=T-1, [x=X,y=Y]]` and `prev.y s + next.y s` at context `[time=T-1, [x=X,y=Y]]`.

Each of the N^2 simultaneous demands for values of `s` at different points for the same `time`-context are evaluated at the same time. Assuming that all values of `s` from the previous time step are available, each value of `s` from the previous time step (except for the ones on the perimeter) will be used four times to satisfy demands generated in computing the values of the four neighbors.

The values of `avg(s)` can be computed when the four values that are demanded are returned. If `s` at contexts `[time=T-1, [x=X-1,y=Y]]` and `[time=T-1, [x=X+1,y=Y]]` are returned, the value of the subexpression `prev.x s + next.x s` can be computed. Independent of this, if `s` at contexts `[time=T-1, [x=X,y=Y-1]]` and `[time=T-1, [x=X,y=Y+1]]` are returned, the value of the subexpression `prev.y s + next.y s` can be computed. The value of `avg(s)` at context `[time=T, [x=X,y=Y]]` can be computed when values of both these subexpressions are available.

It is also possible for two demands, `s` at contexts `[time=t+1, [x=k,y=l]]` and `[time=t, [x=i,y=j]]` to be satisfied simultaneously if the values that they demand at the respective previous time steps are available. This could be the case provided `abs(k-i)` > 1 and `abs(l-j)` > 1.

Since we have considered exploitation of parallelism at the computing model level, we have ignored any impact of any practical implementation resource limitations such as fixed number of processors, limited communication bandwidth, and non-uniform memory access latency.

Sorting Example

The sorting program (which we saw first in Chapter 1) possesses a hybrid form of parallelism that we call tournament parallelism. It combines temporal parallelism with spatial parallelism in a structured manner.

```
sort.u(A, n) =
  realign.w,u B @ log n
    where
      dimension w;
        B = (A fby.w eod) fby
            merge.w(firstOfPair.u(B),
                    secondOfPair.u(B));
        firstOfPair.v(C) = C @.v (# * 2);
        secondOfPair.v(C) =  C @.v (# * 2 + 1);
        merge.a(x, y) =
          if iseod yy or xx <= yy then xx
                                  else yy fi
            where
              xx = upon.a(x, iseod yy or xx <= yy);
              yy = upon.a(y, iseod xx or yy < xx);
           end;
        upon.a(x, p) =
          x @.a q
            where
```

```
                q = 0 fby.a if p then q + 1 else q fi;
            end;
        end
```

Assume that a list of size 4 is being sorted (i.e., n=4) which means log n = 2. Assume that initially sort.u(A,n) is demanded at context [u=0], which causes realign.w,u B @ log n to be demanded at context [u=0, w=0, time=0]. This causes B to be demanded at context [u=0, w=0, time=2]. This, in turn, causes B to be demanded (through merge)) at contexts [u=0, w=0, time=1] and [u=1, w=0, time=1] simultaneously. (We are assuming that merge is pointwise with respect to dimension u, which is, in fact, the case.)

Demand for B at [u=0, w=0, time=1] causes B at [u=0, w=0, time=0] and [u=1, w=0, time=0] to be demanded simultaneously. This causes A at the same contexts to be demanded simultaneously. Similarly, demand for B at [u=1, w=0, time=1] causes A at [u=2, w=0, time=0] and [u=3, w=0, time=0] to be demanded simultaneously.

Assuming all values of A (and thus B at time=0 are available as input, the function merge is applied twice simultaneously, one with values of B at contexts [u=0,w=0,time=0] and [u=1, w=0, time=0], and the other with values of B at contexts [u=2, w=0, time=0] and [u=3, w=0, time=0]. This results in the values of B at contexts [u=0, w=0, time=1] and [u=1,w=0,time=1] to be produced simultaneously. Function merge at [u=0, w=0, time=2] can be applied resulting in the value of B to be produced at the same context. This is, in fact, the desired result that was originally demanded, namely, sort.u(A,n) at context u=0.

The degree of parallelism is at its maximum when the time-context is 0—if there are n elements, there are n/2 simultaneous comparisons. At each successive stage, the number of simultaneous comparisons reduces by a factor of 2 until the last stage when there is no parallelism. (Note that the number of comparisons at each stage is $O(\mathtt{n})$.) Sorting a sequence of n elements using eduction would take linear time assuming at least n/2 processors and constant communication latency and uniform memory access latency.

6.2 Fault Tolerance

Fault tolerance is the ability, by redundancy, to provide dependable service in spite of faults occurring or having occurred [31]. The two principal types of hardware faults are omission faults and corruption faults [41]. Omission fault is caused by the failure of a hardware component such as a processor, a memory module, or a communication link. Its effect on an application being executed is the sudden and complete loss of information resulting in the application being non-functional. Corruption fault is caused by the malfunction of an operational hardware component. Its effect on application being executed is the inadvertent modification of information resulting in incorrect functionality of the application.

The two common techniques for fault tolerance are temporal redundancy (recompute what failed after fault is detected) and spatial redundancy (simultaneously compute the same result and use majority voting to distinguish the correct result from the faulty or corrupted one). Such redundancy can be incorporated at any level of abstraction from the lowest hardware level to the high programming level.

Fault tolerance is usually incorporated at the hardware level; this insulates the application software from needing to explicitly detect and recover from effects of hardware faults. However, hardware-level fault-tolerance is architecture-specific and varies considerably from architecture to architecture even though the application software may be the same. It is desirable to make fault tolerance a property of the application software regardless of the underlying hardware. This has been the objective of techniques such as recovery blocks and N-version programming. These techniques are explicit in that it is up to the programmer to explicitly incorporate fault tolerance into applications.

With `Lucid` programs, fault tolerance can be an implicit property. This is possible by augmenting the eduction model of computation. Each correct yet differing implementation of this augmented model of computation will fault-tolerantly evaluate `Lucid` programs. We now discuss the origin of fault tolerance in evaluating `Lucid` programs.

6.2.1 Origin of Fault Tolerance

The fault tolerance property of the intensional computing model, eduction, was discovered serendipitously by Lee and Jagannathan while testing the first implementation of the abstract architecture for eduction [32]. The implementation directly reflected the abstract architecture where each component was a process and the connections between components were implemented using queues. Using this implementation, it was possible to evaluate `Lucid` (circa 1984) programs. And a standard `Lucid` benchmark to test any implementation of `Lucid`, sequential or otherwise, was a program to compute the digits of e using a simple but subtle algorithm. A property of the program that is worth noting here is that its evaluation makes considerable use of the variable value component in storing new variable values and retrieving previously computed variable values as successive digits of e are computed.

When the benchmark program was evaluated using the implementation, something peculiar occurred, which, at first, seemed like an inefficiency in the implementation. What was observed was that the rate at which digits of e were being generated degraded exponentially. Moreover, this was not characteristic of the program itself but of its behavior when evaluated using the this particular implementation. To determine the cause, a careful trace of the implementation was conducted. It resulted in the discovery of a bug in the implementation of the variable value component: when a variable value was computed and stored, the associated flag that indicated that the value had been computed and was subsequently available was inadvertently never set. This caused subsequent demands for the value to look for the value in the variable value component, not find it, and recompute the value as if it was being computed for the first time. The value was eventually computed except it had to be computed from scratch since none of the other values it used were stored. This explained why the program got exponentially slower with time. More and more of the variable values that had been computed earlier were needed and each of them had to be recomputed each time from scratch.

What was intriguing about this was that the program despite the presence of the bug actually worked although much slower than expected. It turned out that it was the demand-driven realization of the intensional eduction model that allowed those and only those values to be recomputed that were inadvertently "lost." And this fault tolerance was not designed into eduction—it manifested itself serendipitously.

We now discuss why a system for executing `Lucid` programs can naturally provide for fault tolerance [25]. To do so, we first discuss the "roles" the language and the computing model play and then consider an example in detail.

6.2.2 Role of Lucid

Lucid, being a functional language, is referentially transparent. This property of Lucid gives an opportunity for both spatial and temporal redundancy, which are the basis for providing fault tolerance. In particular, referential transparency ensures that, in general, two occurrences of the same subexpression in a program denote, or will evaluate to, the same value. This property ensures that evaluating an expression several times, even if it really occurs only once, will always yield the same value. (It is easy to see that features that destroy referential transparency, such as side effects and aliasing, destroy this multiple evaluability property.) These multiple evaluations can either occur simultaneously (spatial redundancy) or at different times (temporal redundancy).

Lucid, being an intensional language, means there are no connected (monolithic) data structures. Data structures are completely distributed and each value of a data structure is tagged (with its context) to indicate its conceptual position in the structure. Importantly, a value can be accessed directly using only the name of the variable and the context. This means that repeated or multiple computations of a value can be done with only the minimum amount of computing, and importantly, without the need for unrelated computations.

It is the fact that Lucid is both functional and intensional that allows both temporal and spatial redundancy to be efficiently incorporated.

6.2.3 Role of Eduction

The key property of eduction that facilitates tolerance of faults is that it is demand driven. A demand for a value causes further demands to be propagated, one for each of the arguments that the value-defining operator needs.

In the presence of omission faults, a demanded argument value may never be produced since either the propagated demand itself may have been lost or the argument value that was produced may have been lost prior to the operator being executed.

Each demand can be augmented with a simple "timeout" mechanism that enables the demand to suspect a omission fault if the demand has not been satisfied by the timeout. Furthermore, a demand can confirm or confute its suspicion by retracing the propagation of the original demand to check if the argument value is still being produced as evidenced by the presence of a suspended operation, which in turn, is awaiting for its arguments. If an omission fault is confirmed, recovery at the model level simply requires the lost value to be redemanded. (Note that referential transparency guarantees that the value that is recomputed will be correct and intensionality guarantees that there is no superfluous computation.)

In practice, it is sufficient to augment only certain demands with the timeout mechanism to reduce the overhead of fault tolerance. One way of achieving this is to identify operations in the program that will attempt to detect faults using timeouts and act accordingly. The length of the timeout itself would have to be tuned to minimize time of detection of an omission fault from when it occurs and subsequent recovery while limiting the overhead of timeout management.

In the presence of corruption faults, a demand (including its context) or the value (including its context) that is produced could be modified. When a demand itself is corrupted, it could manifest as an omission fault if the demand itself is unrecognized as a demand. It could also manifest in a value at a different (unintended) context to be computed if the demanding context is corrupted. When this value arrives at the suspended operation, the corruption could be noted by comparing the context of the value with the context at which it was demanded. The only case that can go undetected is when the value is corrupted but the context is correct.

This can be detected using the spatial redundancy technique, which can be quite simply incorporated into eduction. In principle, all that is needed is that demand for a value be replicated and the redundancy of a demand be noted using a separate field associated with the value. (The field can be part of an augmented context.)

In practice, it is sufficient to employ redundant demands at certain "critical" points of the program. This would mean that detection of and recovery from a corruption fault would take somewhat longer but the amount of redundant computation would be substantially reduced.

6.2.4 Fault-Tolerant Eductive Evaluation

Consider evaluation of the Laplacian relaxation example we considered earlier in the presence of an omission fault. Demand for the value `s` at context `[time=T, [x=X,y=Y]]` causes `avg(s)` to be computed at context `[time=T-1, [x=X,y=Y]]`. This, in turn, causes demands for `prev.x s + next.x s` at context `[time=T-1, [x=X,y=Y]]` and `prev.y s + next.y s` at context `[time=T-1, [x=X,y=Y]]`.

Without loss of generality, assume that the latter demand is lost due to an omission fault. Only demands for the values of `s` at contexts `[time=T-1, [x=X-1,y=Y]]` and `[time=T-1, [x=X+1,y=Y]]` are issued. When produced, these values would cause value `prev.x s + next.x s` to be produced at context `[time=T-1, [x=X,y=Y]]`. However, value `prev.y s + next.y s` at context `[time=T-1, [x=X,y=Y]]` would not be produced unless it is demanded again.

This can be accomplished as follows: Demand for `avg(s)` at context `[time=T, [x=X,y=Y]]` after a sufficient amount of time checks if any of the outstanding demands, namely, demand for `prev.y s + next.y s` at context `[time=T-1, [x=X,y=Y]]`, is still being processed in which case it waits for some more time. If there is no evidence of the demand being processed, which is in fact the case with the particular fault scenario, it reissues the demand and awaits for the value to be produced this time. Eventually, the value will be produced causing the value `avg(s)` at context `[time=T-1, [x=X,y=Y]]` to be produced, which, in turn, causes value `s` at context `[time=T, [x=X,y=Y]]` to be produced.

In the above example, the same process would be required even if the demand that was lost was actually processed and resulted in a value that got lost before satisfying the demand.

Consider now a corruption fault where the demand for value `s` at context `[time=T-1, [x=X, y=Y+1]]` is corrupted. The resulting value of `s` at context `[time=T, [x=X,y=Y]]` would be incorrect when produced.

The effect of such a corruption fault can be tolerated by issuing redundant demands when processing certain demands. For example, we could have demand for `s` at context `[time=T, [x=X, y=Y]]` result in three identical demands for `avg(s)` at context `[time=T-1, [x=X, y=Y]]`. (The identical demands could have a field identifying themselves in the context.) Each of these demands result in demands for values of `s` at context `[time=T-1, [x=X-1,y=Y]]`, context `[time=T-1, [x=X+1, y=Y]]`, context `[time=T-1, [x=X, y=Y-1]]`, and context `[time=T-1, [x=X, y=Y+1]]`. Even if one of the demands for `s` at context `[time=T, [x=X,y=Y]]` results in an incorrect value due to corruption, the other two would result in the correct value (assuming no other corruption faults). The correct value can be decided by majority voting.

6.3 Summary

In this chapter, we have shown that `Lucid` programs can express different forms of parallelism commonly found in applications including functional, temporal, and spatial parallelism. The expression of parallelism is not only succinct but it is implicit. And the eduction model can naturally exploit all three forms of parallelism.

We have also shown that `Lucid` programs facilitate fault tolerance due to their referential transparency and intensional nature. Both temporal and spatial redundancy can be easily augmented to eduction causing swift detection and efficient recovery from the effects of omission and corruption faults.

Chapter 7

High-Performance Implementation

In Chapter 1, we saw how `Lucid` could be used to express solutions to standard problems such as sorting and matrix multiplication. One of the unique characteristics of `Lucid` is not only that it can be used as a programming language but it can also be used as a "composition" language. That is, instead of using `Lucid` to specify computations, it can be used to express how computation components (expressed in some other language) can be "glued" together to form a coherent application. By doing so, the resulting application can enjoy some of the practical benefits attributable to `Lucid` such as high performance through exploitation of implicit parallelism and robustness through software fault tolerance.

In this chapter, we discuss one such use of `Lucid`—as part of a hybrid language to construct parallel applications to be executed on conventional parallel computers.

7.1 Conventional Parallel Programming

A conventional parallel computer either consists of a number of processors each with local memory interconnected by a network (as in distributed memory architectures) or a number of processors that share memory possibly using an interconnection network (as in shared memory architectures). The past decade has seen the advent of conventional parallel computers starting with the Denelcor HEP evolving to the CM-2 and Intel Hypercube and further evolving to the CM-5, Intel Paragon, Cray T3D, and IBM SP-2. Even networks of workstations (or workstation clusters) are seen as low-cost ("poor man's") parallel computers.

Programming of conventional parallel computers has proven to be far more challenging than had been expected. Part of the reason is the continued use of low-level, explicitly parallel programming models such as `PVM` [42], `Linda` [10]. Two factors have fueled the continuing use of such languages despite their limited success.

1. The need to reuse existing sequential code because the cost of rewriting legacy applications from scratch is considered prohibitive both in economic and technical terms.

2. The need to run on conventional parallel computers that view a "parallel program" at a low level—as consisting of sequential processes that frequently synchronize and communicate with each other using some form of message passing.

The low-level operational approach to programming conventional parallel computers has placed additional responsibilities on the programmer. The programmer is not only responsible for conceiving a parallel solution (in the form of an algorithm), but is also burdened with several aspects of parallelism management such as load distribution (deciding where to send which process), scheduling (deciding the order in which activities need to be distributed), synchronization (knowing when two processes are in compatible states), and communication (specifying how two processes will exchange information). None of the issues of parallelism management have anything to do with the problem solution per se—they are mostly to do with how to effectively implement a parallel solution on a particular computer. Even the higher-level languages for programming conventional parallel computers (such as `HPF` [21] and `PCN` [11]) that hide many of the low-level details typically require parallelism to be specified explicitly.

7.2 Hybrid Parallel Programming

Although the low-level operational approach to programming conventional parallel computers unnecessarily burdens the programmer, the high-level declarative approach (as espoused by the language `Lucid`) cannot, in general, be efficiently compiled to such computers. Besides, there is great resistance to reprogramming existing imperatively-specified applications in a purely declarative language.

What is needed is a hybrid language—one which combines high-level implicit specification of parallelism with low-level explicit specification of computation. This way parallelism management is handled implicitly and existing sequential code is reused.

This is precisely the basis for the language GLU (pronounced "glue", short for Granular Lucid) invented by Jagannathan and Faustini [28, 27]. A GLU program consists of a declarative part (in Lucid) and an imperative part. The declarative part specifies the program in terms of data dependencies between user-defined functions. These (sequential) functions are specified imperatively using existing code fragments.

We illustrate the hybrid nature of GLU using a mergesort program and relating it to the Lucid version discussed in Chapters 1 and 6.

The GLU definition of mergesort function sort is given below.

```
sort.u( A, n) =
  B @.time log n
    where
      B = A fby.time
             merge( firstOfPair.u(A),
                    secondOfPair.u(A));
      firstOfPair.v(C) = C @.v (#.v * 2);
      secondOfPair.v(C) =  C @.v (#.v * 2 + 1);
   end;
```

The essential difference between the above definition and the earlier Lucid definition is the manner in which sorted sublists are represented. Recall that in the Lucid definition, sorted sublists are simply eod-terminated sequences in an orthogonal dimension w.

In GLU, sorted sublists are stored as extensional sequences thus eliminating dimension w. In particular, variable A is a u-sequence of w-sequences in the Lucid version and a u-sequence of foreign objects (lists) in the GLU version.

Similarly, in the Lucid version, variable B is also a u-sequence of w-sequences except that the u-sequence shrinks with increasing time-contexts while each of its w-sequences grows with increasing time-contexts. In the GLU version, variable B is simply a u-sequence of foreign objects (lists), which shrinks with increasing time-contexts. The lists themselves grow with increasing time-contexts although this is not apparent from the definition itself.

In the Lucid version, function merge merges two sorted w-sequences using intensional operators such as upon. In the GLU version, function `merge`, which is defined *imperatively*, merges two sorted lists to return a single sorted list.

The hybrid nature of GLU is reflected in the manner in which the processing is partitioned between the declarative (intensional) part and the imperative (extensional) part. The declarative part only specifies the parallel structure of the sorting algorithm (i.e., a one-dimensional tournament). The imperative part (C function `merge`) expresses the mergesort computation itself. Thus, the leaves of the tournament are extensional lists of size one that are merged into sorted extensional sublists of size two. In general, each interior node of the tournament at a given level denotes an extensional sorted sublist obtained by merging two extensional sorted sublists of half the size from the preceding level.

The program also illustrates a certain duality between extensional and intensional programming. In the Lucid version of mergesort, sorted subsequences are `eod`-terminated sequences in an auxiliary dimension (`w`) and the final sorted sequence are realigned from the auxiliary dimension to the dimension of the original sequence using the intensional function `realign`. In the GLU program, sorted subsequences in an auxiliary dimension are extensionally represented as sorted sublists, which to the intensional part of GLU program appear as uninterpreted values (i.e., list pointer addresses). It is the imperative part, through function `merge`, that directly deals with list pointer addresses.

The other way in which Lucid and GLU programs differ is in the granularity of parallelism they express. Parallelism in Lucid programs is at the level of the individual operations, and thus fine grain. Parallelism in GLU programs varies in granularity depending on the execution time of imperatively specified functions such as `merge`, which doubles with each level of the tournament after initially being fine grain.

7.3 GLU Programming System Architecture

The main goal of GLU is to enable programming of conventional parallel computers without being burdened by operational details. We now discuss how a GLU program is translated into target-specific executables and, in doing so, point out the benefits of GLU.

Figure 7.1 shows the architecture of the GLU system. The system consists of three layers: a programming layer, an virtual execution

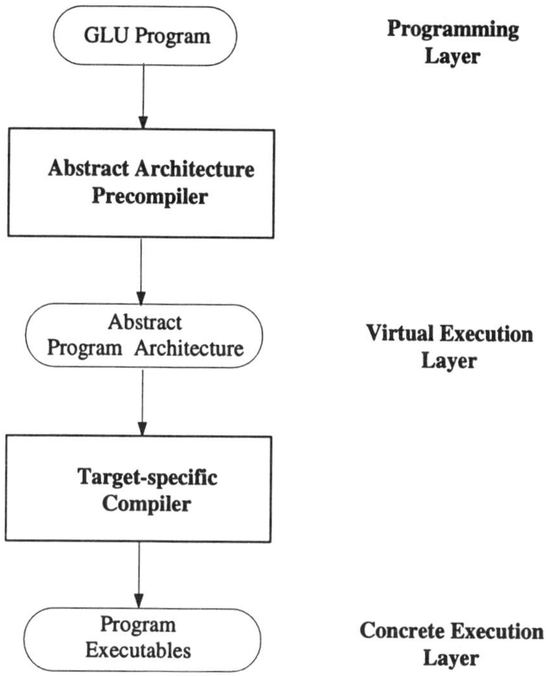

Figure 7.1: Architecture of the GLU System

layer, and a concrete execution layer.

A GLU program is at a sufficiently high level that it is independent how the program will be evaluated on a specific parallel computer. While there are many ways in which it can be evaluated, the GLU program has primacy over all these different ways in terms of the program functionality.

Let us consider how a GLU program is compiled to target-specific program executables. A GLU program is first mapped onto an abstract architecture that specifies how the program will be evaluated using a set of interacting processes. This mapping is provided by the abstract architecture precompiler. And the mapped program is referred to as an abstract program architecture.

The abstract program architecture is compiled to program executables using a target-specific compiler. The compiler translates each process of the abstract program architecture into target-specific object code and implements the inter-process communication and synchronization interfaces of the abstract program architecture using target-specific libraries.

Abstract Program Architectures

An abstract architecture not only specifies how parallelism implicit in a GLU program is to be exploited (for example, using eduction) but also specifies how to schedule executable functions, where to distribute them, and even how to handle failures. When a GLU program is precompiled, it is translated to an abstract program architecture that is an instantiation of a particular abstract architecture. We describe two abstract architectures: a master/worker architecture and a complete peer architecture. Figure 7.2 shows both the master/worker and the complete peer abstract architectures.

The master/worker architecture consists of a master (M) and several workers (W). The master implements eduction—it emulates demand propagation, fine-grain operation execution, result collection, and storage. It also executes those sequential functions that cannot be remotely executed either because they are not coarse-grain enough or because they need to be local. The master uses the workers to execute sequential functions using their arguments, producing results that are returned back to the master. The parallelism exploited is in the concurrent execution of these sequential functions by the multiple workers running on multiple processors. The granularity of parallelism depends on the execution time of sequential functions relative to the communication time taken to send arguments and receive the result. The load distribution strategy for the master/slave architecture is dynamic; that is, each worker waits on the master to assign a sequential function to execute and waits again upon returning the result. The master/slave architecture can tolerate failure of any worker whether it be blocked on the master or in the middle of executing a sequential function when failing. (This assumes that sequential functions behave idempotently.) Furthermore, the master/slave architecture can accept addition of workers at any point in the computation. This architecture is limited in performance because there is an upper limit on the number of workers that a master can keep busy with work. This limit depends on a number of implementation factors such as the bandwidth available between master and workers, the overhead associated with demand propagation and value storage management. The architecture has limited fault tolerance because it cannot tolerate the failure of the master itself.

The complete peer architecture addresses these limitations on scalability and fault tolerance. It consists of several peers (P) that

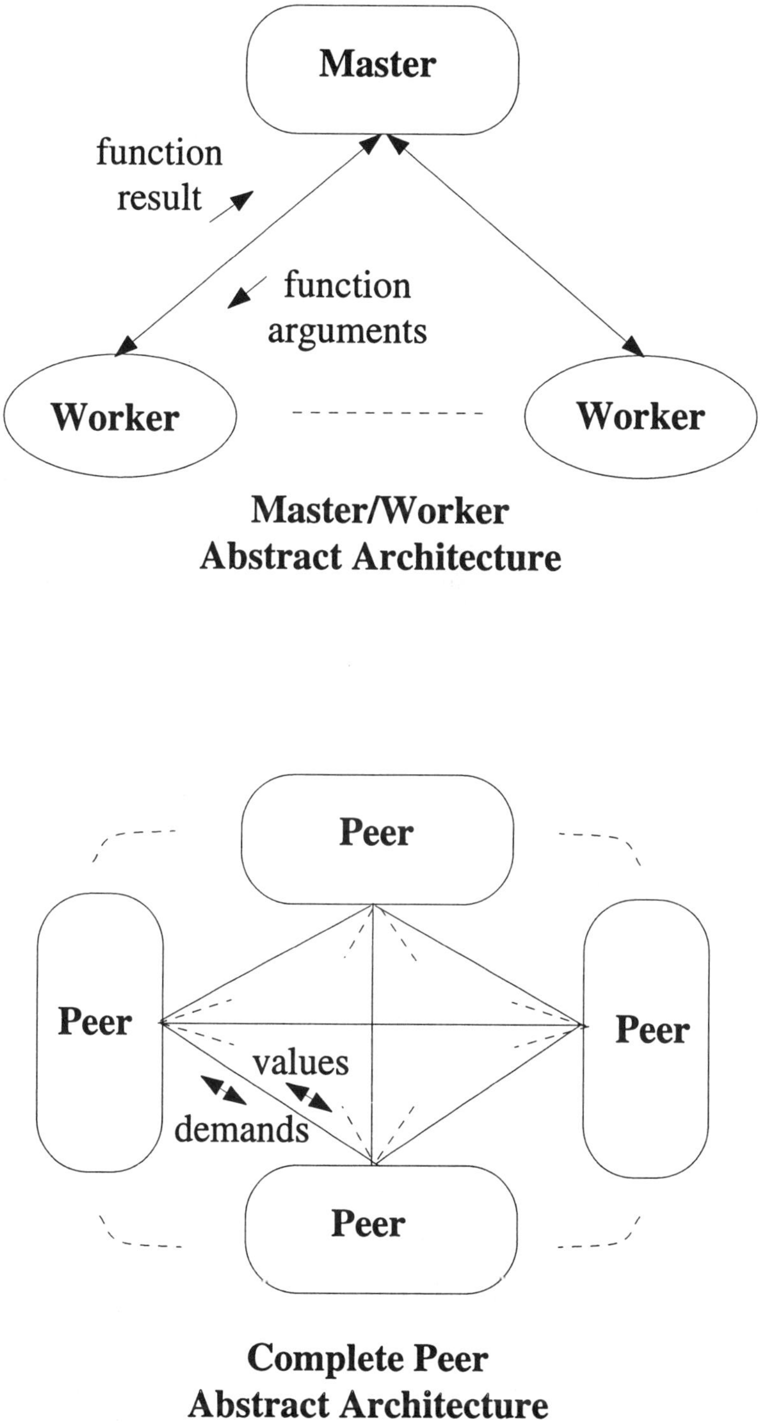

Figure 7.2: Abstract GLU Program Architectures

are fully interconnected with inter-peer latency being variable since it depends on the underlying target architecture. Demand propagation, fine-grain operation execution, result collection and storage, and sequential function execution are distributed across the peers. Parallelism is exploited in the simultaneous execution of coarse-grain functions by the different peers. The load distribution across peers is achieved by applying a hash function to demands for tagged values. Assuming enough implicit parallelism in computations, performance of the architecture can be scaled by addition of peers. The architecture can tolerate failure of peers (since other peers can "take over").

Each abstract architecture offers a unique strategy for parallelism management. The most suitable abstract architecture for a given program depends not only on the characteristics of the program but also on the kind of conventional parallel computer on which it will run. For example, the master/worker architecture is quite suitable for programs whose granularity of parallelism is quite coarse and which will be executed on workstation clusters or uniform shared-memory parallel computers. On the other hand, the complete peer architecture is suitable for programs that have requirements for fault tolerance and which will be run on hypercube-based architectures.

Target-Specific Program Executables

The generation of program executables for a specific target parallel computer depends on the abstract program architecture itself. The structure of the executables would reflect the underlying abstract architecture. With the master/slave abstract program architecture, the executables will consist of a master process and a worker process. With the complete peer abstract program architecture, the executables will consist of identical peer processes.

Abstract program architecture can be implemented on target-specific basis. For example, on a shared-memory parallel computer, the interaction between processes of an abstract program architecture can be implemented using semaphores or portable mechanisms such as the ones provided by `Linda`. On a distributed-memory parallel computer, this interaction can be implemented using native message passing mechanisms or portable mechanisms such as `PVM`.

7.4 Revitalizing Existing Applications

One of the main criticisms of declarative languages in general is that they are almost never used to program "real" applications. We address this valid criticism by showing how GLU has been used to program three practical applications from different areas. Each GLU application has been derived from its sequential equivalent while largely reusing existing sequential code and writing very modest amounts of Lucid code. This evidence of rapid conversion of existing code is crucial when dealing with large sequential legacy applications[1].

7.4.1 Ray Tracing

The first application we consider is ray tracing. The basic idea is construct an observer's two-dimensional image of a three-dimensional scene given fixed light sources. This has been implemented using a 5000 line sequential C program. The ray tracing algorithm used in this program is such that the color of each point of the image can be computed independent of any other point. Thus, the application is inherently highly data parallel.

We can express the application in GLU as follows

```
SCENE in( int );
IMAGE display( IMAGE );
IMAGE trace( SCENE, POSITION, POSITION );
IMAGE juxtapose( IMAGE, IMAGE, IMAGE, IMAGE );

image where
  image = planar_tree.x,y( juxtapose,
                           display( trace( scene, x, y ) ),
                           xdim*ydim )
          where
            dimension x, y;
          end;
  scene = in(time);
end
```

The GLU program for ray tracing uses four components: `in`, `display`, `trace`, and `juxtapose`. Each of these components have well-defined interfaces: `in` for each invocation returns a scene description

[1]The largest sequential legacy application that has been parallelized using GLU is a 400,000 line message handling server written in C. The conversion only required approximately 0.5% of changes to the sequential code. See [29] for more details.

of type `SCENE`. `display` accepts an image of type `IMAGE` and returns a the same image after displaying it; `trace` accepts three parameters, namely, the scene to rendered of type `SCENE`, and the Cartesian coordinates of the point in the image (of the scene) to be traced and it returns a single-pixel image of type `IMAGE`; `juxtapose` accepts four adjacent images and composes an image from these four images that it returns as its result. The data types `STATUS`, `IMAGE`, `SCENE`, and `POSITION` are assumed to be defined in C.

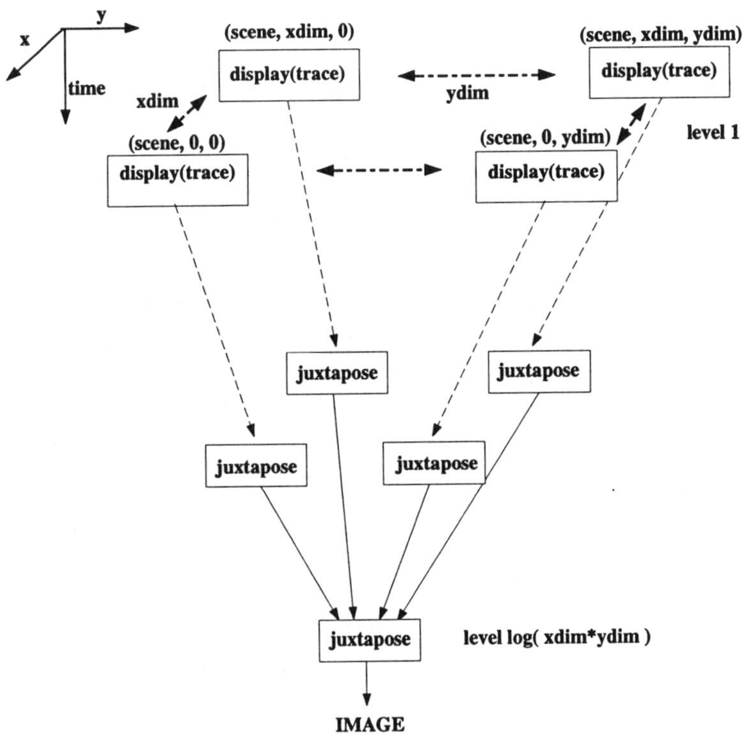

Figure 7.3: Ray Tracing in GLU

The Lucid-level composition specification for ray tracing reflects its simple yet highly parallel structure. The goal is to display the observer's image (as in `display( image )`. The variable `image` itself is defined using the GLU function `planar_tree` over dimensions `x` and `y`. This function defines a pyramid structure (or a planar tree) whose base is of size `xdim * ydim` and whose depth is log_2(`xdim*ydim`). The structure of the pyramid is such that the number of points of a layer are a quarter of the layer above. The first argument specifies how each point of an interior layer is to be constructed from four neighboring points of the layer above. In the example, function `juxtapose` is used to compose an image at each point of layer from four neighboring images from the layer above. The second argument specifies how the points of the base layer of the pyramid are to be computed (and displayed). In the example, each point corresponds to a single-pixel image that is constructed by applying `trace` to the scene for that particular point. The third argument specifies the size of the base of the pyramid. In the example, it is given as `xdim*ydim` where `xdim` and `ydim` are assumed to be constants.

It is important to note that each point of a layer including the base can be computed independent of any other point of the same layer and that successive layers need to be computed sequentially. The data parallelism is in the simultaneous computation of each point of a layer. The degree of data parallelism is `xdim * ydim` initially and it reduces by 4 for each successive layer until there is only one image (at the tip of the pyramid). Figure 7.3 illustrates the parallelism in this application.

The granularity of parallelism is defined by the complexity of function `trace`. The granularity can be made coarser by associating each point of the pyramid base with a block of pixels instead of a single pixel. Furthermore, the pixels in a block do not have to be adjacent and this can be taken into account by `juxtapose`.

We were able to "parallelize" the sequential ray tracing application in a matter of days with less than 50 lines of changes even though we had not written the original sequential program. This not only confirms our view that GLU enables rapid conversion of existing code but also suggests that many sequential applications have a natural and often simple parallel computation structure. The next application, in structural engineering analysis, originally designed in the Civil Engineering department of Arizona State University, further confirms the above observation.

7.4.2 Structural Analysis

The analysis of the majority of structural engineering systems tends to be inherently complex in nature. The simplified examples usually found in textbooks are not often found in actual design situations. As a result, a true structure is generally replaced by an idealized approximation suitable for mathematical analysis. Establishing the structural idealization that approximates the true structure remains a prime problem for the structural engineer.

Normally the structural idealization of surfaces is obtained by subdividing the original continuum into a number of plate elements bounded by intersecting lines. It is common practice to replace the original continuum by an assemblage of rectangular finite elements, then, by recurring to a matrix-displacement analysis, the true displacement field of the continuum is approximated by the displacement of the finite elements. We assure ourselves that the displacements are sufficiently accurate by applying the most general convergence criterion for the finite element approach, which states the following.

> The total energy of the substitute system obtained by assembling finite elements must approach that of the original when the number of elements is increased without limit.

During the last twenty years the request for more detailed analysis of large and complex structural systems composed of several thousands of these elements has become common practice. Such detailed analysis requires large order finite element models and excessive demands in computations and data management.

Therefore, an efficient implementation of the algorithm on a high-performance computing system, using GLU, could potentially deliver the kind of detailed analysis that structural engineers have hitherto believed to be unattainable at a reasonable cost [35].

Efficient use of the resources of a high-performance computing system can be achieved if separate processing elements are held responsible for a given subdomain, In other words, each processing element will be assigned a part of the structural system and charged with the assembling and computing of its substructure stiffness matrix. Once a processor element has computed its assigned substructure stiffness matrix and has solved for its corresponding flexibility matrix at its locality, it will only need to return the contributions of its assigned substructure to the global system. Under this paradigm, a single processor element generates its own sub-system rigidity matrix, calculates its flexibility matrix, then proceeds to compute a flexibility matrix made up by the degrees of freedom corresponding to the nodes that are boundary nodes to the rest of the structural system. In order to complete its work, each processing element needs to create the appropriate mapping of its substructure's local boundary degrees of freedom to match the global system degrees of freedom. Finally it will forward this information to the processing element (or processing elements) in charge of compiling/collecting the global system flexibility matrix. It is important to note that the collection of the work done by the processing elements is also in parallel. And, of course, after all simultaneous collections are completed the combined information will become the flexibility matrix of the global structural system.

Most existing major structural analysis applications were designed 10 to 20 years ago and have been optimized for current sequential computers. Such applications, and the algorithms they embody, are neither well structured nor formulated to take maximum advantage of advances in parallel computing technology. With `GLU`, it is possible to implement new formulations of parallel solutions while reusing much of the existing sequential code.

Below is the `GLU` program that implements the structural analysis of a box girder bridge. The C functions `topplate`, `botplate`, and `webplate` as well as `put` and `add` are extracted directly from the original sequential application. The basic data structure is `MATRIX`, a 2-dimensional matrix of type `double`. The result of executing the program is a display of the total structure using function `display`.

```
#define  pi 3.14159
#define  elmd 3.e+7       /* Modulus of Elasticity */
#define  pois 0.25        /* poisson ratio */
#define  blen 60.0        /* Length of Bridge */
#define  ants 0.*pi/180.  /* angle of top slab */
#define  anbs 0.*pi/180.  /* angle of bottom slab */
#define  answ 90.*pi/180./* angle of slab to left web */
#define  wilo 16.0        /* width of left overhang */
#define  wiro 16.0        /* width of right overhang */
#define  dlwe 10.0        /* depth/length of left web */
#define  celw 20.0        /* typical cell width */
#define  nelo 2           /* number of finite elements
                             across left overhang */
#define  nero 2           /* number of finite elements
                             across right overhang */


struct matrix
   {
        int x, y;
        double v[x][y];
   };
typedef struct matrix *MATRIX;

MATRIX put( MATRIX,int,int,int);
```

```
int display(MATRIX);
MATRIX add( MATRIX, MATRIX );

MATRIX  topplate(int,double,double,double,double,
                 double,double,int,int,int,int,int,
                 int,double,double,double,double);
MATRIX  webplate(int,double,double,double,double,
                 double,double,int,int,int,int,int,
                 int,double,double,double,double);
MATRIX  botplate(int,double,double,double,double,
                 double,double,int,int,int,int,int,
                 int,double,double,double,double);
int input(int);

display(t) fby.time eod
where
  nelb = input(0);
  ncel = input(1);
  nepc = input(2);
  nepw = input(3);

  power_of_two = #.time asa.time width == 1;
  width = ncel + 3 fby.time (width+1)/2;

  t = tree @ power_of_two
  where
    dimension i;
    tree = b fby
           if width % 2 == 0
              then add(tree, next.i tree)
              else tree fby.i add(tree, next.i tree)
           fi @.i (2 * #.i);

    b =  if plate <= ncel+3
            then put(bridge,plate,ncel,nelb)
            else eod fi;
    plate  = i+1;
    bridge = if (plate == 1) then
                topplate(plate,elmd,pois,blen,wilo,
                         wiro,celw,nelb,nelo,nero,ncel,
                         nepc,nepw,ants,answ,anbs,dlwe)
             elseif (plate <= ncel+2) then
                webplate(plate,elmd,pois,blen,wilo,
                         wiro,celw,nelb,nelo,nero,ncel,
                         nepc,nepw,ants,answ,anbs,dlwe)
             elseif (plate == ncel+3) then
```

```
                    botplate(plate,elmd,pois,blen,wilo,
                             wiro,celw,nelb,nelo,nero,ncel,
                             nepc,nepw,ants,answ,anbs,dlwe)
                else eod fi;
    end;
  end
```

The main source of parallelism in the above program is tournament parallelism. At the base of the tournament are simultaneous invocations to one instance of **topplate**, several instances of **webplate**, and one instance of **botplate**. At each successive level of the tournament, the results (i.e., matrices) from the previous level are added together using add until only one result remains, which is displayed. The parallelism is initially $O($**ncel**$)$ and subsequently geometrically decreases to 1.

The GLU system has allowed the new (parallel) formulation of the structural analysis problem to achieve a complexity of over 20,000 degrees of freedom. This places the implementation in the range of performance of supercomputers and dedicated parallel processing systems for such problems. But what has been the most impressive result is that this high performance throughput using GLU has been achieved using inexpensive high-performance Unix workstations.

7.4.3 Intrusion Detection System

Finally, we consider an application that is non-scientific in nature but one that typifies a large class of "data processing" applications. The application called IDES for "Intrusion Detection Expert System" is used to detect intrusive and suspicious activity on computer systems [33]. The computer systems being monitored are called "target" systems. They generate audit trail of all user activity on the system. The audit trail is transmitted by each target system, as it is generated to IDES.

We chose to "gluify" the IDES application because the performance and scalability of sequential IDES is limited by the computational power of the underlying system that it runs on.

The IDES application itself consists of the three following stages.

1. A collection phase where the audit trails from various target systems are collected and collated by user instead of by target (since a user can be simultaneously using multiple target systems).

2. An analysis phase where the activity represented by the audit trail is analyzed independently by a statistical and a rulebased component and the multiple analysis resolved to determine if the activity is currently suspicious or even intrusive.

3. A presentation phase where any significant events and their analysis are provided to a security-officer for further consideration.

The IDES application consists of the following modules written in C.

```
AuditRecord Collect();
StatsState InStatsState();
RulebaseState InRulebaseState();
Userid User( AuditRecord );
( StatsAnalysis, StatsState )
       Stats( StatsState, AuditRecord );
( RulebaseAnalysis, RulebaseState )
       Rulebase( RulebaseState, AuditRecord );
Analysis Resolver( StatsAnalysis, RulebaseAnalysis );
Status Report( AuditRecord, Analysis );
```

Function `Collect` returns an audit record of type `AuditRecord` from a pool of audit records that are continually generated by the various target systems. Function `InStatsState` returns the initial statistical state of type `StatsState`. Function `InRulebaseState` returns the initial rulebase state of type `RulebaseState`. Function `User` returns the userid (of type `Userid`) in audit record denoted by argument of type `AuditRecord`. Function `Stats` accepts the current state (of type `StatsState`) and audit record (of type `AuditRecord`), applies statistical analysis to the audit record given the currents state, and returns the analysis (of type `StatsAnalysis`) and the new state (of type `StatsState`). Similarly, function `Rulebase` accepts the current state (of type `RulebaseState`) and audit record, applies rulebased analysis to the audit record given the current state, and returns the analysis (of type `RulebaseAnalysis`) and the new state (of type `RulebaseState`). Function `Resolver` accepts both the statistical and rulebased analysis, resolves and augments the analyses, and generates a comprehensive analysis of type `Analysis`. Function `Report` accepts an audit record (of type `AuditRecord` and an analysis (of type `Analysis`), presents, if necessary, an anomaly report to the security officer, and returns a status of type `Status`.

It is instructive to describe the sequential IDES application using these modules.

```
StatsState ss[ USERS ];
RulebaseState rs[ USERS ];
Userid u;

for each user u
  {
    ss[ u ] = InStatsState();
    rs[ u ] = InRulebaseState();
  }

while( TRUE )
 {
   AuditRecord ar;
   StatsState newss;
   RulebaseState newrs;
   StatsAnalysis sa;
   RulebaseAnalysis ra;
   Analysis as;
   Status status;

   ar = Collect();     /* Get next audit record */
   u  = User( ar );    /* userid */
   /* perform statistical analysis */
   Stats( sa, newss, ss[u], ar );
   ss[ u ] = newss;
   /* perform rulebase analysis */
   Rulebase( ra, newrs, rs[u], ar );
   rs[ u ] = newrs;
   as = Resolver( sa, ra ); /* resolve */
   status = Report( ar, as );  /* report */
 }
```

Note that each audit record is processed fully before the next audit record. Also, for a given audit record, the various phases (collection, analysis, and presentation) are performed serially. Furthermore, within the analysis phase, `Stats` processing is completed before `Rulebase` processing.

The most obvious form of parallelism inherent in IDES is in the analysis phase where each audit record can be simultaneously processed by both the statistical and the rulebased components. This kind of parallelism is referred to as *function parallelism* and it is usually evident in examining the static processing structure of the application (i.e., Figure 7.4).

A less obvious form of parallelism inherent in IDES is in the simultaneous execution of the collection phase, the analysis phase (and within it, execution of statistical/rulebased components at the same time as the resolver component), and the presentation phase. This kind of parallelism is referred to as *temporal parallelism* and it is evident by examining the temporal nature of the IDES application.

While both function and temporal parallelism when exploited could speed up the IDES application, the speedup is limited by the average number of independently executing components in the case of function parallelism and by the number of stages in the processing pipeline of IDES in the case of temporal parallelism. This is fundamentally limited by the static structure of the application.

What is desirable is for the performance of the IDES application to "scale" with the number of users being monitored. In fact, this is possible by simultaneously processing audit trails of distinct users that are is collated by the collection phase of IDES. This way the analysis of an audit record from each of the audit trails can proceed in parallel. We refer to this kind of dynamic parallelism as *spatial parallelism.* Furthermore, this parallelism is orthogonal to the function and temporal parallelism discussed earlier. The granularity of parallelism is coarse since the grain size corresponds to the complexity of the collection phase, the analysis components, and the presentation phase.

We now consider how the IDES application can be expressed using the GLU model thus expressing the inherent parallelism we identified above. (This is pictorially shown in Figure 7.4.)

```
Report( ar, as )
where
  ar  = Collect();
  as = multi.u( analyze, ar, User( ar ) ) where
       dimension u;
         analyze( ar, u ) = Resolver( next.time sa,
                                      next.time ra )
           where
             ( sa, newss ) = Stats( ss, ar )
               where
                 ss = InStatsState()
                      fby.time newss;
               end;
             ( sa, newrs ) = Rulebase( rs, ar )
               where
```

```
                    rs = InRulebaseState()
                         fby.time newrs;
                  end;
              end;
           end;
   end
```

Note that the first argument to **multi** is **analyze**, which is the name of a function thus making **multi** monopomorphically higher order. It is similar to **planar_tree** that we saw earlier in this respect. Also note that two of the equations in the above program each define two different variables, instead of one. This is merely for syntactic convenience in GLU as the righthand sides of the two equations each return two values to positionally match the two lefthand side variables.

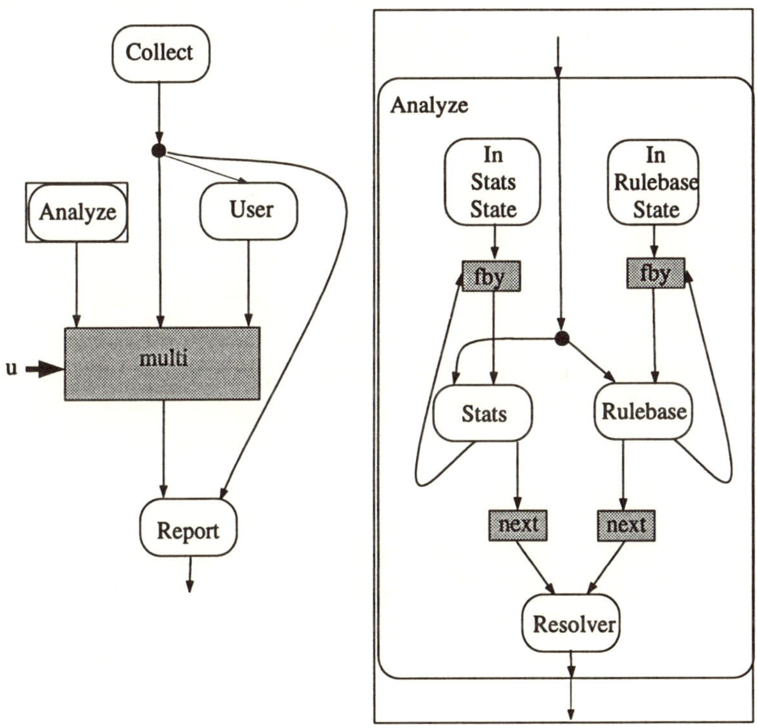

Figure 7.4: IDES in GLU

Function **Collect** is used to gather audit data from various sources where it keeps them sorted by userid. Dimensionally abstracted function **multi** enables audit records belonging to different users to be processed independent of one another while ensuring that successive audit records of a given user are processed in order. For each audit record (or set of audit records) of a given user, function `analyze` is applied which causes both `Stats` and `Rulebase` to be simultaneously applied. The result of these two functions is processed by `Resolve` and passed onto function `Report` for appropriate display.

The main source of parallelism is the ability to process audit data streams belonging to different users simultaneously. In addition, the ability to process `Stats` and `Rulebase` simultaneously is an example of function parallelism and pipeline parallelism is exploited in the simultaneous operations of the collection, analysis, and reporting phases of `IDES`.

In migrating the IDES application to run in parallel, we have been able to retain much of the original sequential code because the design was highly modular. In general, modular sequential applications can be more effortlessly parallelized using `GLU` than poorly designed applications.

7.5 Summary

We have described how `Lucid` has been used as part of a hybrid language called `GLU` for programming conventional parallel computers. We first described the `GLU` model of programming and then considered the architecture of the `GLU` programming system. We then illustrated the benefits of GLU by showing how it has been used to *revitalize* three "real" applications, namely, ray tracing, structural engineering analysis, and an intrusion detection expert system. The benefits of `GLU` include the ability to rapidly convert sequential applications to parallel equivalents with minimal amount of changes and to the ability to efficiently execute the converted applications on a wide range of conventional parallel computers [26]. At SRI, with Chris Dodd as the principal implementor, `GLU` has been successfully implemented on heterogeneous workstation clusters, symmetric multiprocessors, and the CM-5.

Chapter 8

Other Uses of Intensionality

In Chapter 2 we presented what is essentially a creation myth of intensional programming—that far-sighted researchers studied intensional logic and then applied this knowledge by designing a language that embodied intensional principles. In fact, the whole project grew out of a more modest attempt to make fairly conventional Pascal-style programming mathematically acceptable. Indexed sequences were originally added so that programs which, in Pascal, used for-loops and reassignment, could be rewritten as equations involving temporal operators.

For example, the "nonmathematical" Pascal loop

```
term := 1; sum := 1;
for i := 1 to 20  do
 begin term := term/i; sum := sum+term end;
e := sum;
```

could be expressed declaratively as

```
i = 1 fby.time i+1;
term = 1 fby.time term/i;
sum = 1 fby.time sum+term;
e = sum as_soon_as.time i eq 20;
```

The indices were simply loop counters—a very mundane application of temporal logic.

The real development of intensional programming began when we noticed that there were equational programs that did not correspond to Pascal loops; and that, more significantly, there were user-defined functions (the nonpointwise ones) that did not correspond to Pascal functions and procedures.

These "nonstandard" programs could not be easily understood in terms of the usual assignment/imperative view of programming—a dataflow model was often more relevant. But their semantics was easily expressed in terms of the basic concepts of intensional logic: intensions, which are maps from a set U of possible worlds to a data domain D; and intensional operators, which map intensions to intensions. Intensions are therefore elements of the domain D^U, and intensional operators are elements of $D^U \to D^U$.

In other words, intensional programming is like extensional programming except that the data domain D (the domain of extensions) is replaced by the domain D^U of intensions, and that the function domain $D \to D$ (the domain of extensional functions) is replaced by the domain $D^U \to D^U$. Notice that in each case the larger domain is really an *extension* of the smaller one, because in each case every element of the smaller domain can be coerced, in an obvious way, to an element of the larger domain. An extensional object $d \in D$ is coerced to the intension $\lambda u d$, and the extensional function f is coerced to the pointwise intensional function $\lambda X \lambda u f(X_u)$.

Intensional programmers are therefore dealing with much richer notions of data and functions. Furthermore, the definitions just given make no assumptions about the universe U of indices (possible worlds)—this opens up even more possibilities. Finally, the characterization just given, of the difference between intensional and extensional programming, is independent of any particular programming language or paradigm. Intensional programming is therefore not inherently linked with functional or even declarative programming, although in practice declarative systems are the easiest to "intensify."

In this chapter we review some of the recent work that explores the possibilities of intensional programming in the general sense just described.

8.1 Intensional Logic Programming

The two main declarative paradigms are functional and logic programming. The Lucid project could be described as the intensification of functional programming; it is only natural, therefore to consider intensifying logic programming.

This process is surprisingly straightforward, in terms of both syntax and semantics, provided we restrict ourselves to the "pure" subset of Prolog.

By pure Prolog we mean "logic programming" in a very literal sense of the phrase: programming in the Horn logic subset of first order logic. In this pure Prolog (which could also be called "Horn Logic Programming") the program statements are Horn clauses; that is, implications in which one atomic formula (the *head* of the clause) is implied by a (possibly empty) conjunction of atomic formulas (the *body* of the clause). Any variables are (implicitly) universally quantified.

For example, the following Horn clause

```
grandfather(G,K) :- father(G,P), parent(P,K).
```

states that for all G, K, and P, if G and P are related by the predicate (relation) father, and P and K are related by the predicate parent, then G and K are related by the predicate grandfather. (We are using the standard C-Prolog syntax.)

Horn Logic Programs can also have compound terms, built up from atoms and variables using operations symbols ("functors"). The following clauses assert that anything constructed from the atom using the operation s is a number, and anything built up from the atom nil and "numbers" using the operation cons is a "numberlist".

```
number(0).
number(s(N)) :- number(N).
numberlist(nil).
numberlist(cons(N,L)) :- number(N), numberlist(L).
```

Pure Prolog does not allow equations between terms; there is no way to say that two different terms have the same denotation and are interchangeable in all contexts. As a result, the "functors" act as constructors—s constructing the natural numbers from 0, and cons constructing lists from nil. (Practical implementations have more convenient and efficient ways of handling arithmetic and list manipulation.)

Pure Prolog has no input/output per se; instead, the user submits (in the simplest case) a query consisting of an atomic formula, possibly with occurrences of variables. If the query is a *ground* formula (has no variables), the implementation attempts to derive the query from the program. If a derivation is found, the query is said to "succeed", otherwise it "fails". If the query contains variables, the implementation should incrementally produce an exhaustive enumerations of all the ground substitution instances of the query that can be derived from the program. In practice, implementations are usually incomplete: there are queries that should succeed, but instead result in nontermination. On the other hand, these implementations usually (though not always) detect failure and report it.

The semantics just given is proof-theoretic and therefore basically operational; in fact, `Prolog` interpreters are really top-down theorem provers, using some variation of resolution. However, there is also an equivalent model-theoretic semantics, which is basically denotational (a model of a set of formulas is just an interpretation—a relational structure—in which all the formulas are true).

This denotational semantics is based on the fact that every set of Horn clauses (every pure `Prolog` program) has a minimal Herbrand model. A *Herbrand* model is one in which the universe of individuals is exactly the set of all ground (variable-free) terms. In other words, in which every object can be constructed from atoms using operations, with different constructions always yielding different results. And the model is *minimal* in the sense that every individual fact (ground atomic formula) true in the model is true in *every* other model.

It can be shown, then, that a ground query to a program succeeds if and only if it is true in the minimal model. More generally, the set of ground instances of a query that succeed corresponds exactly to the set of all assignments of values to the variables that make the query true in the minimal model.

Notice that we just described Horn Logic programming in terms of purely logical concepts, such as "proof" and "model"—this is why we call it "pure" `Prolog`. And now that we have characterized the language in purely logical terms, it is relatively easy to give the generalization to intensional logic.

The basic idea is to retain Horn logic, but to move from ordinary extensional logic to intensional logic. In ordinary logic, a relational structure consists of a domain and an indexed family of relations, one for each predicate. For convenience, let us define a relation to be a boolean-valued function, so that (for example) a binary relation is in the domain $(D \times D) \rightarrow B$, B being the boolean domain.

To move to intensional logic, we choose a nonempty universe U of possible worlds and extend our relations so that their *truth values* vary from one world to another. Thus a binary relation now denotes an element of $(D \times D) \rightarrow (U \rightarrow B)$ or, equivalently, of $U \times (D \times D) \rightarrow B$. Notice that this is a much more modest extension than is the case with functional programming, where D itself is replaced by $(U \rightarrow D)$, so that U appears on both sides of the arrow. There are serious unsolved technical difficulties with a more ambitious extension, to be discussed later. Also, the more modest extension chosen corresponds exactly to Kripke's semantics for modal logic.

In terms of syntax, we extend the language by adding intensional operators that are applied to *formulas* (and not terms).

As a very simple example of intensional Horn logic programming, we can take U to be the set of natural numbers, and extend the language by allowing the two unary operators `first` and `next` to be applied to formulas in Horn clauses. The result is a temporal logic programming language that Wadge and Orgun call `Chronolog`.

In `Chronolog` we can write Horn clauses which describe how a system changes with time. Consider the program

```
first light(green).
next light(red) :- light(green).
next light(green) :- light(red).
```

The first clause says that `light(green)` is true at time 0. The other two say that if `light` succeeds with one color at time t, it succeeds with the other color at time $t + 1$. Thus the query `first next next light(green)` succeeds, as does `first next next next light(X)` with `X = red`.

Notice that the three clauses above, considered as a complete program, define the unary predicate `light` to be *single-valued*: at any time t, `light(X)` succeeds for exactly one value of `X`. Single valued predicates can therefore be thought of as representing *streams*; in this case, the stream $<$ `green, red, green, red,` $\ldots >$.

The following `Chronolog` program defines the predicate `nat` to represent, in the same way, the stream of all natural numbers

```
first nat(0).
next nat(s(N)) :- nat(N).
```

And this program defines `fib` as the representative of the stream of all Fibonacci numbers:

```
first fib(0).
first next fib(1).
next next fib(Z) :- fib(X), next fib(Y), sum(X,Y,Z).
```

(here `sum` is a the predicate form of the addition operation). [36] presents more interesting applications, including a `Chronolog` formulation of the Dining Philosophers problem. For example, the rule

```
next act(P,eat) :- act(P,eat), hungry(P,yes).
```

states that a philosopher who is currently eating, but still hungry, will continue eating.

Naturally there is no need to restrict U to be the set of natural numbers. In particular, we can have multidimensional Horn logic programming with analogs of `first` and `next` in each dimension. Orgun and Wadge have shown that the model theory of Horn logic programming carries over to intensional logic programming. In the general case we must put certain restrictions on the kinds of operators that may appear in programs. The Intensional approach can also be extended to "don't care" nondeterminism, by allowing programs that have many different *minimal* models, but not necessarily a single unique *minimum* model.

Early attempts to define a `Lucid`-analog of `Prolog` used a stronger notion of intensional relation, one in which the arguments, as well as the truth value, varied in time. By this we mean letting (say) binary predicates denote objects in $(U \to D) \times (U \to D) \to (U \to B)$. If U is the set of `Lucid` time points, this gives us a language in which we have predicates *of stream*, not just simple ordinary `Prolog` objects. The problem, however, is implementation: answering a query involves constructing an infinite object. We can do this incrementally, of course, but in the presence of nondeterminism we can never be sure of *any* part of the answer—at any point in time, we may have to backtrack all the way to the beginning. This stronger notion of intensional logic programming is therefore inherently unimplementable.

The same problems do not arise in connection with the weaker notion described here. In the case of `Chronolog`, for example, a unary predicate represents essentially a stream of sets of finite objects, not a set of streams of finite objects. The individual sets in the stream can be enumerated one by one, independently. In fact, if we choose some obvious rules for `first` and `next`, a simple extension of the usual resolution method can form the basis for a `Chronolog` interpreter [36].

8.2 Branching Time

In the original `Lucid` language, the index domain (the set of natural numbers) was thought of as a set of time points—`Lucid` was designed as a *temporal* functional programming language.

Of course by choosing the set of natural numbers as the set of time points we are at the same time choosing a very simple model of time. In this model there is a first instant, and every instant has a unique successor. This is the bare minimum required to formulate conventional iterative constructs.

The intensional paradigm, however, has no commitment to any particular model of time or to any corresponding particular set of timepoints. This would suggest investigating temporal programming based on a different notion of time.

In this section we examine the consequences of dropping the assumption that each timepoint has a unique successor. Instead, we will allow (some) timepoints to have multiple incomparable successors. We will also assume that the descendents of distinct timepoints remain distinct, so that the set of all timepoints forms a *tree*.

This notion of *branching time* may seem counterintuitive, but it is mathematically simple and has been well studied by logicians. And, as we shall see, it has already proved to be very useful from the intensional programming point of view.

Let us begin with the simplest branching time model, one in which every instant has exactly two uniformly distinguishable successors. The set of timepoints then forms a binary tree. If we let `0` denote the first successor and `1` the second, every timepoint is uniquely identifiable by a binary sequence. The first digit in the sequence identifies which successor of the starting timepoint was taken, the second, which successor of the successor, and so on. The *length* of the boolean sequence corresponds to the linear notion of "elapsed" time.

We can easily adapt the traditional linear-time primitives (`first`, `next`, and `fby`) to binary branching time. The operator `first` is unchanged, because there is still a unique initial timepoint. Instead of a single `next`, however, we need two: `next0` and `next1`. Finally, we still have only a single `fby` operator, but it must take *two* right-hand arguments.

If we identify the timepoints with the corresponding binary sequences, we can give the formal semantics of these operators as follows:

$$
\begin{aligned}
(\mathtt{first\ X})_s &= \mathtt{X}_\epsilon \\
(\mathtt{next0\ X})_s &= \mathtt{X}_{s0} \\
(\mathtt{next1\ X})_s &= \mathtt{X}_{s1} \\
(\mathtt{A\ fby\ (X,Y)})_\epsilon &= \mathtt{A}_{epsilon} \\
(\mathtt{A\ fby\ (X,Y)})_{s0} &= \mathtt{X}_s \\
(\mathtt{A\ fby\ (X,Y)})_{s1} &= \mathtt{Y}_s
\end{aligned}
$$

Here are simple iterative branching time definitions

```
N = 0 fby (N+1, N+1);
S = 0 fby (S, S+N);
```

The first defines `N` to be a simple counter: `N` is initially 0, and on each step it is increased by 1, no matter which choice is made. The second defines `S` to be a running sum of the values of `N`, except that the current value of `N` is added to `S` only when we take the second branch. Thus, for example, the value of `S` at the timepoint corresponding to the sequence 0110101 is 13, because 13 = 1+2+4+6.

One way of understanding branching time programs is to think of them as *nondeterministic* iterative programs. For example, we can understand the definition of `S` as saying that `S` is initialized to 0, and that on each step `S` *either* remains the same *or* has the current value of `N` added on, depending on the choice made.

Branching time is useful in writing search programs—in particular, binary searches. A good example is the "knapsack" problem: we are given a list `L` of natural numbers, and we must discover if a target number `T` is the sum of a sublist of `L`. Here is a branching time program for the knapsack problem.

```
first F
where
 K = L fby (tail(K), tail(K));
 W = head(K);

 S = 0 fby (S, S+W);

 F = if S eq T  then true elseif
        S > T   then false elseif
        L eq [] then false else
        next0 T or next1 T fi;
```

The program can be explained quite easily in terms of nondeterministic iteration. The definitions of K and W arrange that W enumerates the elements of the list L; after n steps, W is the $(n-1)^{th}$ element of L, no matter which choices have been made.

S is defined as a nondeterministic running sum of the values of W; at each step, W is added to S only if the second branch is taken.

The search of the possibilities will take place during the evaluation of F, which is defined in terms of its own future(s). F will be true at a given timepoint if and only if the target T has been "hit" at that timepoint or at one of the timepoints in the given points future(s). The value of F at the origin is the required result of the search.

Informally, the program determines whether or not, in some possible future sequence of events, the running sum hits the target—or, more precisely, hits the target *before* the list is exhausted. This formulation suggests introducing general-purpose temporal operators for searching backwards and forwards in time, so that the subject of the clause could be replaced by the expression `S eq T before (S > T or K eq [])`. Then `P before Q` could be defined using future recursion, as in the program, or in terms of other general purpose operations, for example as `eventually (P and not hitherto Q)`.

The knapsack problem is usually solved using recursion. This would suggest some connection between (first order) recursion and branching time iteration, and this is exactly the case. In fact, GLU and other Lucid implementations handle recursion by translating it into branching time iteration; in a sense, the tree of function calls is mapped onto the tree of time points.

To see how the translation works, consider the following recursive "schema"

```
F(A)
where
 F(X) = if p(X) then q(X) else h(F(k0(X)),F(k1(X))) fi;
end
```

We can translate it into branching time as

```
first F
where
 F = if p(X) then q(X) else h(next0 F, next1 F) fi;
 X = A fby (k0(X), k1(X));
end
```

Notice that the function *and* its formal parameter both become simple variables varying in branching time. The formal parameter X is no longer bound (a dummy). It now denotes an indexed family of *actual* parameters. The function variable `F` has become a simple variable, which denotes the indexed family of the corresponding results.

P. Rondogiannis has now provided a correctness proof for this translation, and has shown it can be extended to (typed) higher order programs. To translate a third order program, for example apply this procedure once to "de-functionalize" all the functions with second-order parameters. The result is a second order program with branching time. We then eliminate the second order functions, in the same way, using a *new* (orthogonal) branching time dimension. After one more step, we have translated a third order program into a zero order (function-free) program that uses three orthogonal branching time dimensions. The translated program can then be implemented using eduction in the normal way.

Another context in which branching dimensions arise naturally is in the study of *attribute grammars*: an attribute can clearly be formalized as an intension that varies over the (branching) space of all nodes in the parse tree. S. Tao has used this idea as the basis her Intensional Attribute Grammar (IAG) system. The IAG approach has several advantages: the definition language is declarative, the attributes may vary in other dimensions (such as `time`), and the trees can be evaluated using eduction.

8.3 Intensional Spreadsheets

Spreadsheets provide another example of a declarative paradigm that lends itself naturally to the intensional approach.

A spreadsheet is, in the simplest case, a rectangular array of "cells", each displaying either a number or some text (a heading, a label). They were originally developed (before the arrival of computers) as a standard form for the presentation of financial information.

	C0	C1	C2	C3	C4
R0		Pat	Chris	Erin	Total
R1	Breakfast	7.85	6.95	6.95	21.75
R2	Lunch	0.00	12.15	11.98	24.13
R3	Dinner	15.23	17.00	10.05	42.28
R4	Total	23.08	36.10	28.98	88.16

The computer spreadsheets automated the process of creating a spreadsheet by allowing the user to explicitly declare relationships between the contents of cells. They do this by allowing the programmer to enter *formulas* in certain cells-formulas which express the content of the cell in question in terms of the values stored in other cells. (Even cells that contain data can be considered as holding formulas consisting of the appropriate constants.)

A spreadsheet *program* is therefore an array of formulas, and the spreadsheet interpreter evaluates the formulas and displays the results. Thus the display above could have been produced by a program that has, for example, the formula `R2C1+R2C2+R2C3` in cell `R2C4`.

Thus, it should be clear that both a spreadsheet program and its output (the display) are *already* intensions. They vary in the horizontal and the vertical "space" dimensions. We can use this view of spreadsheets as intensions to design an intensional expression language that is both simpler and more general than the usual ad hoc notations used by existing commercial systems.

The intensional language is, in the simplest case, just the subset of `Lucid` in which the only dimensions are `hor` and `ver`, and the only variable is `S`—an explicit name for the whole display. In each cell the programmer places an expression which, when evaluated at the context corresponding to the cell, produces the desired value.

For example, consider again the cell `R2C4` in the above example. We want it to display the sum of the contents of the three cells to the left. In our intensional language, the formula

```
pre.hor pre.hor pre.hor S + pre.hor pre.hor S + pre.hor S
```

works. In fact, the intensional version is more general, because we can use exactly the same expression in the other cells in the fourth column. In spreadsheet jargon, the intensional version is *relative* because it refers to other cells according to their position in relation to the cell in question, and not in relation to the home cell `R0C0` of the sheet.

Of course, the commercial spreadsheet systems also have ad hoc relative notations; for example, `R+0C-3 + R+0C-2 + R+0C-1` might denote "the sum of the three cells to the left." Conversely, in the intensional language, we can formalize absolute references using the `first` operators. For example, `R0C1` corresponds to the intensional expression `first.hor first.ver next.ver S`.

The intensional language, however, is much more general because we can put *any* expression in a cell, not just one built up using data operations applied to individual cell references. And these expressions can use built-in or user-defined functions, including nonpointwise functions. For example, suppose we have a built-in function `left(i)` that returns the value of `S` i steps in the negative `hor` direction. Then we can use the expression `left(3)+left(2)+left(1)` in the cells in column 4.

Better yet, we can define a dimensionally abstract function `sum.d( i,j )` that returns the sum of the cells in the ith through the jth positions (relative to the cell in question) in dimension `d`. The expressions in the fourth column can then be condensed to `sum.hor(-3,-1)`, and those in the fourth row can be `sum.ver(-3,-1)`.

The `sum` function could be built-in, or it could be defined by the user, say as

```
sum.d(i,j) = tot asa.e #.e > j-i
  where
   dimension e;
   tot = 0 fby.e tot + S @.d (#.d+i+#.e);
  end;
```

The understanding is that these function definitions are global, that is, not just valid in one particular cell.

One obvious extension to this intensional spreadsheet is to other global dimensions, besides `ver` and `hor`. The simplest case is to add `time` (as an implicit dimension)—then a sheet becomes a `time`-varying rectangular array of data items. The user interface could be designed to take this interpretation of the `time` dimension into account, say by providing commands for stepping through the stages of the iteration.

We can still have a *single* defining formula for each cell. The programmer can use temporal operators to specify the way the values change with time—and so avoid writing separate formulas for each cell in each "layer" of the time dimension.

For example, suppose that the sheet given above is just one layer of a three dimensional expenses record, with a layer for each day. We can extend the program so that row 5 has a running total of expenses *to date*; for example, so that on day 3 cell `R5C2` displays the total expenses for Chris (see table on Page 142) up to and including that day. We simply enter the formula

```
first.time pre.ver S fby.time S + next.time pre.ver S
```

Alternatively, we can use our generic `sum` function and enter the formula `pre.ver sum.time(0,#.time)`.

Other extensions are possible as well. We could allow multiple sheets in the same program, possibly defined through mutual recursion. No special linking mechanism is required—we just allow defining formulas of `S` to refer to sheet (say) `T`, and vice versa. These extra sheets need not be defined cellwise—we could allow the user to specify them with a single, global equation. For example, the equation

```
T = (sum.ver(-1,+1) + sum.hor(-1,+1) - 2*S)/4;
```

defines each cell of `T` to be the average of the values of the immediate neighbors of the corresponding cell of `S`.

Another possibility is a *nested* or *hierarchical* spreadsheet: one in which some cells can be opened up to reveal an entire spreadsheet; some of whose cells in turn reveal subsubsheets, and so on. A nested spreadsheet would allow structured spreadsheet programming, with the details of subcomputations hidden from view, not just shoved off to a "remote" area. Nesting corresponds to enlarging the context space to include arbitrarily long finite *sequences* of pairs of integers. The expression language would have the usual operators plus extra level-switching operators for accessing (say) the parent cell, or cells in a subsheet.

One big advantage of the intensional spreadsheet is that they can be evaluated using eduction—lazily, in an incremental, demand-driven fashion. To calculate the value of `S` at a particular cell (and particular time) we fetch the cell's expression and demand its value at the given context. This translates into demands for other values of `S` (or other sheets) at other cells and timepoints, some of which may already be computed and are found saved in the (associative) variable-value store. There is therefore no need to analyze the program, calculate dependencies, and devise some sequential evaluation order.

W. Du and W.W. Wadge have already designed and implemented an intensional spreadsheet [15, 16]. Recently M. Stadelmann produced a variant that uses nondeterministic constraints, rather than expressions [40], and Q. Wu describes one in which sheets are both nested and time-varying. Only the Du/Wadge implementation is eductive, and all are just prototypes—there is as yet no commercial product based on these concepts.

8.4 Multiple Dimensions

It should be clear from the previous sections in this chapter, and indeed from previous chapters, that intensional programming has evolved and developed primarily by adding additional dimensions. Originally, there was only one dimension, the `time` dimension. Extra time dimensions were added to handle nesting, and then space dimensions were incorporated to allow an intensional approach to arrays. User-defined functions were originally a problem until C. Ostrum discovered how to remove them from the source at the cost of adding a branching time dimension. Later, we discovered (as described above) that higher order programs could be "de-functioned" in the same way using extra branching time dimensions. Tao's intensional attribute grammar system is based on an intensional language with a `tree` dimension, the points of which are nodes in a parse tree. This system also has a time dimension for iterative attribute calculations, and a `name` dimension for the intensional treatment of aggregate values in which the parts are indexed by identifiers. Finally, all of the intensional systems can be adapted to handle version control by adding a version dimension to those already present.

It should come as no surprise that the extra dimensions cause implementation problems that did not arise with the original one-dimensional language. In fact, we already face a serious problem when we add a single extra dimension (say, a space dimension `s`). The cause of our difficulties is that first-principle semantics dictates that every intension in the two-dimensional language is a function of a time and a space parameter. This means that every demand will consist of a program variable together with an `s` and a `t` value as will every value that is produced as a result of the demand.

The problem with this is that some variables may in fact be independent of space; the value of such variable at time `t` and point `s` may be function of `t` alone. In that case, we risk wasting a lot of storage space by computing the same value at the same time but different space points. Of course, it could be that the definition of `X` involves complicated calculations and that it just happens that various terms cancel out, so that the value of `s` does not enter into the value of `X`. In that case we cannot expect the implementation to ignore the space tag. On the other hand, it may be completely obvious that `X` is independent of space; say, because it is defined recursively in terms of itself, using only time operations. In that case it should be possibly for the implementation to deduce the fact, and demand and save values of `X` with only the `time` field filled in the tag.

This sort of deduction is what we call *dimensionality analysis.* The dimensionality of an expression or variable is a set of dimensions (dimension symbols) that gives an upper bound on the dimensions to which the denotation of the expression or variable is sensitive. We can calculate the upper bounds by a series of successive approximations. We begin by assuming every program variable has dimension {} (constant). We use this approximation to calculate an upper bound on the defining expressions of the program variables. These new values, which may not all be empty, are used as the second approximation to the dimensionality of the corresponding program variables. The second approximation is used to calculate new upper bounds for the defining expressions, which become our third approximation. We continue the iteration until the values settle down, giving us (it can be shown) a valid upper bound on the dimensionalities of the program variables. These upper bounds can then be used to limit the size of tags and avoid some unnecessary duplication of values.

This process becomes more difficult in the presence of user-defined functions. One approach to dealing with functions is to repeatedly feed dimensionality information through the function bodies. A more efficient approach is to abstract dimensionality information from the body. When the function is higher order, this is more complex. This works with the GLU implementation even though GLU does not have a fixed set of dimensions. In fact, a GLU program can have finitely many dimensions which can be handled by renaming. The renaming approach breaks down when there are infinitely many dimensions as can be created by nested time operators and recursive dimensionally abstract functions. This breakdown is caused by the breakdown of eduction itself—it seems to require infinite tags. One solution to this is based on the observation that with infinite dimensions, the contexts *themselves* are intensions—a multitime point is an intension over the time metadimension, a metadimension being the index set of a family of related dimensions. This suggests that the contexts themselves be computed lazily (i.e., on demand using the lazy tags approach). In this model, the tag is not sent out with the demand. Instead, the demand for the variable is sent and the eductor replies with questions about the context—each answer being the value of the context at a given dimension. After a finite dialogue, enough information has been gathered about the context to compute the value of the variable at that context (which has locally finite dimensions).

The snag is, what tag should this value be stored with? We can attach the record of the dialogue but how will we know where to look the next time? Different values will be stored with different tags, and there maybe no way *a priori* to predict what tag will be attached to a value we seek. There is a solution for intensions that are *functionally sequential* in terms of contexts. Roughly, this means that as the dialogue proceeds, either we already have a value, or there is one definite dimension we must ask about next. These intensions have a kind of decision tree, which can be stored incrementally in the value warehouse. With each tag (partial dialogue) we store *either* the value of the intension *or* the next dimension to enquire about. Although this scheme has not yet been implemented, it is very general and should handle almost any program—the familiar operators (`first`, `next`, `asa`, etc.) are all functionally sequential.

8.5 Intensionality and Inheritance

It is impossible to talk about programming "paradigms" without bringing Object Oriented (OO) programming to mind. The question therefore arises, is there any relationship between Intensional Programming (IP) and OO programming?

There is in fact a close relationship, but this relationship was not uncovered in the obvious way, by adding intensional operators to an OO language. Instead, it grew out of an (initially ad hoc) attempt by one of the authors (Wadge) to manage a family of prototype implementations of various intensional systems.

Originally, IP meant programming in One Big Language (`Lucid`). Implementing IP therefore meant implementing *the language*. Soon after the publication of the `Lucid` Book [45], however, we gave up the attempt and began developing a whole family of languages and systems based on intensional logic. The language `Lucid` that we have described in this book is still the most prominent member of this family, but not the only one. In fact, the main objective of this current chapter is to give some idea of the diversity that is already apparent in the intensional family—spreadsheets, logic programming, attribute grammars, higher order languages, and so on.

One great disadvantage of having a family of systems is that you need a family of implementations. We have been lucky to find a whole family of talented graduate students/implementors (Du, Rolston, Mitchell, Orgun, Tao, Wu, Stadelmann, Dodd, Lee, and many others). Their efforts, however, have realized only a fraction of the possibilities. Each single paradigm has many variations—temporal logic programming with branching time, or with user-defined dimensions, multidimensional spreadsheets, infinite branching time, etc. Some of these variants may be more useful than others, but we may never know which are the useful ones until we try them out.

We would obviously need whole regiments of graduates to produce separate implementations, even prototype implementations, for all these possibilities. Fortunately, there is also no *need* to produce separate implementations, because these systems really are members of a family, and have strong family resemblances. Instead, we can (incrementally) build a family of implementations in which related members *share* code that implements common features. For example, all the spreadsheet systems might share the display procedures, and all the `Lucid`-like functional languages would share the code for implementing branching time.

In other words, the alternative approach is to view the various implementations as *versions* (variants) of a single piece of software. We therefore need an approach to version management and configuration that allows code sharing between versions. Obviously, this is an important problem not limited to software which implements intensional systems. In fact almost all important commercial products (computers, copiers, airplanes, automobiles, lately even books and newspapers) exist in versions. The control and configuration of the related software and documentation is already a serious problem.

The intensional approach to version control is based on two simple observations.

The first is that a family of variants of a piece of software can be thought of as an *intension*, one which varies over a context space whose possible worlds are the particular versions.

The second observation is that a piece of software is the result of combining its components, and that this combination process is a pointwise operation. In other words, we configure the (say) `french` version of a word-processor by assembling the `french` versions of its basic components.

These observations are, by themselves, not much help, because they seem to rule out sharing between related versions. Most likely (especially if the software is designed) there will only be a few modules for which the `french` version is different from the standard one. It is wasteful and error-prone to require the programmer to produce separate `french` copies of every module.

Instead, we can establish a default convention: if no separate `french` version of a module `M` can be found, then the `french` version of `M` (the value of `M` at the `french` world) is the *same* as its standard value (its value at the `standard` world). Conceptually, then, `M` is still an intension with an extension at each world; but the programmer does not actually have to create separate labeled copies of each extension.

The configuration process is only slightly more complicated. To configure the `french` version, we assemble all the required modules, in each case taking the one labeled `french` if it exists, otherwise taking the one labeled as standard.

The principle involved becomes clear once we introduce subversions; for example, with `french%quebec` and `french%guadaloupe` as subversions of `french`, which (along with, say, `german` and `italian`) is a subversion of `standard`. When configuring the `french%quebec` version we try, for each module, to find an explicit `french%quebec` version. If none exists, we look for a separate `french` version; and if that is not available either, we take the `standard` version.

The principle is that if there is a copy of a module `M` labeled with a version α, but none labeled with immediate subversion β, then $\mathtt{M}_\beta$ is taken to be equal to $\mathtt{M}_\alpha$. In other words, by default the β version of the whole system *inherits* its components from those of version α. In general, to configure version α of the system, we examine, for each module `M`, the set of all subversions γ of α for which a labeled copy of `M` exists (we call these γ the *relevant* versions of `M`). If this set has a least element (least in the subversion ordering) then we take that version of `M`; otherwise there is an error condition. We can summarize the procedure by saying that we assemble system by choosing, for each module, the *most relevant* version of that module.

In [38], Plaice and Wadge describe a simple version management system (`Lemur`) for `C` software based on the intensional approach. `Lemur` allows sharing of object code as well: it keeps track of the versions used in compiling a `.o` file, and attaches the appropriate tag. The system allows multiple inheritance: the sum $\alpha+\beta$ of versions is a subversion of both α and β. Sums are used to recombine separate versions. For example, the `french+fast` version is the one which is both French *and* fast. When combining the `french` and `fast` versions, the programmers have to consider only those modules which exist in both versions. In these cases, it is necessary to produce an explicit `french+fast` version, for otherwise configuration will fail (neither the `french` nor the `fast` will be the most relevant).

The basic idea behind the `Lemur` approach is to use a partially ordered context space and an inheritance rule as the basis of an economical representation of an intension. The same idea can be applied in other systems in which the program text itself is not monolithic but varies over a context space.

We have already seen, for example, how in the spreadsheet the definition of `S` is given by a whole array of separate expressions, one for each point in the context space. And we have already seen examples where this is uneconomical because all the formulas (say, in a particular row) are identical. We can avoid this problem by introducing extra context points that stand for entire `classes` of cells, and allow the user to give expressions for these classes that will be inherited by the cells in each class.

For example, we can add class-contexts for each row and each column, and one for the entire sheet (with subset ordering). Then to calculate the value at a particular cell, we first check if there is an expression in that particular cell. If there is we evaluate it, otherwise we look for an expression attached to the row or column in which the cell appears. If there is one, we evaluate it, otherwise look for the generic (default) expression attached to the whole sheet. Clearly multiple inheritance arises again, when the classes (considered as sets of cells) overlap. We could forbid them; or we could require that at the point where they overlap, the expressions have the same value.

Context inheritance also works well with attribute grammars, where typically many productions (such as those involving arithmetic operations) all have identical definitions.

Finally, the intensional approach to versions can be fairly easily adapted to allow versioning of software in existing intensional paradigms—the version code is another dimension, although not *just* another dimension, because context inheritance has to be taken into account.

8.6 Summary

In this chapter, we show how the general principle of intensionality finds use in numerous programming models and systems. Its use in logic programming has resulted in temporal logic programming language called `Chronolog`. We have shown how intensionality can accommodate a more general notion of time, namely branching time and how this notion can be incorporated into `Lucid`. One use of branching time is in implementing higher-orderness and another is in attribute grammars. We show that with finite but unbounded multiple dimensions, eduction should not only be used to compute tagged values but to compute the tags themselves. We also outline how applications such as spreadsheets and version control can be significantly enhanced by applying the principle of intensionality.

Bibliography

[1] E.A. Ashcroft. Towards an APL compiler. In *Proceedings of APL6*, Anaheim, California, U.S.A., May 1974. ACM.

[2] E.A. Ashcroft. Ferds—Massive parallelism in Lucid. In *Proceedings of the 1985 Phoenix Computer and Communications Conference*, pages 16–21. IEEE, March 1985.

[3] E.A. Ashcroft. Dataflow and eduction: Data-driven and demand-driven distributed computation. Technical Report SRI-CSL-151, Computer Science Laboratory, SRI International, Menlo Park, California 94025, U.S.A, 1986.

[4] E.A. Ashcroft. Eazyflow architecture. In S.S. Thakkar, editor, *Selected Reprints on Dataflow and Reduction Architectures*, pages 395–432. IEEE Computer Society, 1987.

[5] E.A. Ashcroft. Tournament computations. In *Proceedings Third International Symposium on Lucid and Intensional Programming (ISLIP 90)*, Queen's University, Kingston, Ontario, Canada, 1990.

[6] E.A. Ashcroft, A.A. Faustini, and R. Jagannathan. An intensional parallel processing language for applications programming. In B.K. Szymanski, editor, *Parallel Functional Programming Languages and Environments*, chapter 2. ACM Press, 1991.

[7] E.A. Ashcroft and W.W. Wadge. Lucid, a nonprocedural language with iteration. *CACM*, 20(7):519–526, 1977.

[8] E.A. Ashcroft and W.W. Wadge. The syntax and semantics of Lucid. Technical Report SRI-CSL-146, Computer Science Laboratory, SRI International, Menlo Park, California 94025, U.S.A, 1984.

[9] R.M. Burstall, J.S. Collins, and R.J. Popplestone. *Programming in POP-2*. Edinburgh University Press, Edinburgh, U.K., 1971.

[10] N. Carriero and D. Gelernter. Linda in context. *CACM*, 32(4):444–458, April 1989.

[11] K.M. Chandy and S. Taylor. *An Introduction to Parallel Programming*. Jones and Bartlett Publishers, Boston, Massachusetts, U.S.A., 1992.

[12] W.F. Clocksin and C.S. Mellish. *Programming in PROLOG*. Springer-Verlag, Berlin, 1981.

[13] Thinking Machines Corporation. Introduction to data level parallelism. Technical Report TR86-14, Thinking Machines Corporation, Cambridge, Massachusetts 02142, U.S.A., 1986.

[14] J. Darlingston. A system which automatically improves programs. In *Proceedings 3rd IJCAI*, pages 479–485, Stanford, California, U.S.A., 1973.

[15] W. Du and W.W. Wadge. A 3D spreadsheet based on intensional logic. *IEEE Software*, 7(3):78–89, May 1990.

[16] W. Du and W.W. Wadge. The eductive implementation of a 3D spreadsheet. *Software–Practice and Experience*, pages 1097–1114, November 1990.

[17] A.A. Faustini and R. Jagannathan. Indexical Lucid. In *Proceedings of the Fourth International Symposium on Lucid and Intensional Programming (ISLIP 91)*, Menlo Park, California 94025, U.S.A, 1991.

[18] A.A. Faustini and R. Jagannathan. Multidimensional programming in Lucid. Technical Report SRI-CSL-93-03, Computer Science Laboratory, SRI International, Menlo Park, California 94025, U.S.A, 1993.

[19] A.A. Faustini, Matthews S.G., and Yaghi AG A. The pLucid programmer's manual. Technical Report TR83-004, Computer Science Department, Arizona State University, Tempe, Arizona 85287, U.S.A., Oct. 1983.

[20] A.A. Faustini and W.W. Wadge. Intensional programming. In J.C. Boudreaux, B.W. Hamill, and R. Jernigan, editors, *The Role of Languages in Problem Solving 2*. Elsevier Science Publishers B.V. (North-Holland), 1987.

[21] High Performance Fortran Forum. High performance Fortran language specification. Version 1.0 CRPC-TR 92225, Center for Research on Parallel Computation, Rice University, Houston, Texas, U.S.A., May 1993.

[22] G.F. Hughes and M.J. Creswell. *An Introduction to Modal Logic.* Methuen and Company Limited, London, U.K., 1972.

[23] E. Issacson and H. Keller. *Analysis of Numerical Algorithms.* Wiley, New York, New York, U.S.A., 1966.

[24] R. Jagannathan. A descriptive and prescriptive model for dataflow semantics. Technical Report SRI-CSL-88-5, Computer Science Laboratory, SRI International, Menlo Park, California 94025, U.S.A, May 1988.

[25] R. Jagannathan and E.A. Ashcroft. Fault tolerance in parallel implementations of functional languages. In *Proceedings 21st Annual Fault-Tolerant Computing Symposium*, Montreal, Quebec, Canada, June 1991.

[26] R. Jagannathan and C. Dodd. Preliminary performance of a parallel GLU implementation on a network of workstations. In *Proceedings of the Fifth International Symposium on Lucid and Intensional Programming (ISLIP 92)*, Oakland, California, U.S.A., 1992.

[27] R. Jagannathan and C. Dodd. GLU programmer's guide (version 0.9). Technical Report SRI-CSL-94-06, Computer Science Laboratory, SRI International, Menlo Park, California 94025, U.S.A, July 1994.

[28] R. Jagannathan and A.A. Faustini. GLU: A hybrid language for parallel applications programming. Technical Report SRI-CSL-92-13, Computer Science Laboratory, SRI International, Menlo Park, California 94025, U.S.A, 1992.

[29] Y. Koui, S. Seno, T. Yamauchi, M. Ishizaka, and K Kotaka. Implementation and evaluation of MHS parallel processing. *IEICE*

Transactions on Communications, E77B(11), November 1994. Tokyo, Japan.

[30] P.J. Landin. The Next 700 Programming Languages. *Communications of the ACM*, 9(3):157–166, 1966.

[31] J-C. Laprie. Dependable computing and fault tolerance: Concepts and terminology. In *Proceedings 15th International Symposium on Fault-Tolerant Computing*, Ann Arbor, Michigan, U.S.A., 1985. IEEE.

[32] R. Lee, E.A. Ashcroft, and R. Jagannathan. Emulating the eduction engine. Technical Report SRI-CSL-148, Computer Science Laboratory, SRI International, Menlo Park, California 94025, U.S.A., 1985.

[33] T.F. Lunt, A. Tamaru, F. Gilham, R. Jagannathan, P.G. Neumann, and C. Jalali. IDES: A progress report. In *Proceedings Sixth Annual Computer Security Applications Conference*, December 1990.

[34] J. McCarthy, P.W. Abrahams, D.J. Edwards, T.P. Hart, and M.I. Levin. *LISP 1.5 Programmer's Manual.* MIT Press, Cambridge, Massachusetts, U.S.A., 1962.

[35] E. Moreno. GLU BRIDGE—A structural engineering application in the GLU programming language. Master's thesis, Arizona State University, Tempe, Arizona 85287, U.S.A., 1993.

[36] M.A. Orgun and W.W. Wadge. Theory and practice of temporal logic programming. In L. Farinas del Cerro and M. Penttonen, editors, *Intensional Logics for Programming.* Clarendon Press, Oxford, U.K., 1992.

[37] S.L. Peyton-Jones. *The Implementation of Functional Programming Languages.* Prentice-Hall, 1987.

[38] J. Plaice and W.W. Wadge. A new approach to version control. *IEEE Transactions on Software Engineering*, 19(3):268–276, March 1993.

[39] G. Polya. Induction and analogy in mathematics. In *Mathematics and Plausible Reasoning*, volume 1. Princeton University Press, 1954.

[40] M. Stadelmann. A spreadsheet based on constraints. Master's thesis, University of Victoria, Victoria, B.C., Canada, 1993.

[41] R. Strong. Problems in fault tolerant distributed systems. In *Proceedings of COMPCON Spring 85*, pages 300–306, San Francisco, California, U.S.A., 1985. IEEE.

[42] V. Sunderam. PVM: A framework for parallel distributed computing. *Concurrency: Practice and Experience*, 2(4), December 1990.

[43] R. Thomason, editor. *Formal Philosophy, Selected Papers of R. Montague.* Yale University Press, New Haven, Connecticut, U.S.A., 1974.

[44] D.A. Turner. *Recursion Equations as a Programming Language*, pages 1–28. Cambridge University Press, Cambridge, U.K., 1982.

[45] W.W. Wadge and E.A. Ashcroft. *Lucid, the Dataflow Programming Language.* Academic Press, U.K., 1985.

[46] A. Yaghi. *An Intensional Implementation Technique for Functional Languages.* PhD thesis, University of Warwick, Coventry, U.K., 1985.

Index